TALK TO YOUR Dog

TALK TO YOUR Dog

How to communicate with your pet

SUSIE GREEN

CICO BOOKS
London

First published in Great Britain
in 2005 by Cico Books
32 Great Sutton Street
London EC1V 0NB
© 2005 Cico Books
Text © 2005 Susie Green

10 9 8 7 6 5 4 3 2 1
ISBN 1-904991-16-5

CIP data for this book is
available from the British Library

Artworks by Trina Dalziel
and Philip Hood
Cover design by Jerry Goldie
Graphic Design
Design by Ian Midson

Photographs:
page 7: the Saluki
page 22: the black Labrador
page 38: a wire-haired
dachshund (left) and Irish
Woldhound (right)
page 70: Samoyeds
page 86: Golden Labradors
page 102: Cocker spaniels
page 120: Golden Labrador

Printed in Singapore

Poppy

For all my canine companions, past,
present and future, and the wild
spirit of the wolf which inhabits
their beloved souls.

"The greatness of a nation and its
moral progress can be judged by the
way its animals are treated."
Mahatma Gandhi (1869–1948)

CONTENTS

CHAPTER ONE:

THE ORIGINS
OF THE DOG

"Dog. n. A kind of additional or subsidiary
deity designed to catch the overflow and
surplus of the world's worship."

Ambrose Bierce, *The Devil's Dictionary* (1911)

The puzzle of the domestic dog's ancestry
has exercised the minds of pet-lovers,
Writers, philosophers, and scientists for
thousands of years. Speculation has
abounded, theories have multiplied, until
at the end of the twentieth century, genetics
has irrevocably revealed that all dogs-
from the luxury-loving Pekingese to the
brave-hearted Rhodesian ridgeback-have
evolved from the intelligent, sociable, and
self-sufficient wolf. In this chapter we
examine the evidence that shows how this
metamorphosis has taken place; and we
discover the world's first ever breeds.

Robert Wayne, Professor of Biology at the University of California Los Angeles (UCLA) discovered that the mitochondrial DNA (invaluable in tracking a species' biological ancestors) in seven different dog breeds and the gray wolf were virtually identical, differing at most by 0.2 percent. As mtDNA only reproduces asexually through the maternal line, this means that originally they all came from the same maternal stock—the gray wolf.

As David Mech, the world's leading expert on wolves, puts it: "Wolves are not just wild dogs. Rather, dogs are domesticated wolves." This does not preclude some genetic material from the wolf's other close relatives (see table, p.10) with whom sometimes it quite naturally interbreeds, producing fertile offspring. And of course, humans intervened from time to time by introducing wild blood into domestic stocks to increase hunting ability—as Great Plains American Indians did by periodically mating their dogs with coyotes.

How Did the Wolf Become Man's Best Friend?

Fifty-five million years ago the animals that we now class in the order Carnivora were far less specialized than they are today. However, as the millennia inexorably moved on, different creatures began to fill specialized ecological niches, developing the most useful characteristics as they did so. Felines developed tongues capable of rasping flesh from bone which they chewed carefully, and became ambush predators; canids evolved into co-operative pack hunters, whose teeth tore lumps of flesh from their prey, which were gulped down whole. It took around 45 million years for the wolf to come into being, and almost another ten million for the domestic dog to be curled up at his human's feet.

It would be almost another ten million years before the domestic dog was curled up peacefully at his human's feet.

Although hugely adaptable omnivores, both wolves and humans are at heart ruthless predators competing for the same prey, be it hare or bison, so it is not surprising that they inhabit the same geographical areas or that they eventually developed a symbiotic relationship. Their bones have been found in close proximity from 400,000 years ago, but the exact nature of their relationship remains speculative. For the wolf there were distinct advantages to lurking in the environs of hominid (any member of the primate family *hominidae* which includes man and his fossil ancestors) encampments. They were less likely to be harassed by predators more fearsome than themselves, such as the giant sabre-toothed cats; the pressure of the their 1000-pound-per-square-inch (200kg/cm^2) jaws could easily crack open juicy bones impenetrable to the puny hominids; and there was the added bonus of hominid excreta to devour.

Wolves, dogs, and pigs have far more efficient digestive systems than humans, which allow them to use as food that which humans excrete as waste. Many contemporary people are disgusted when their dogs eat animal excreta or, depending on the environment, human excreta; this behavior, labeled as "having a depraved appetite," means that the poor canine is often roundly chastised. However, although sophisticated urban humans now find this perfectly natural behavior repulsive, we should remember that wolves, dogs, and pigs—both in the past and now in areas such as rural India—have done man a great service by acting as a flesh-and-blood sewage system, a characteristic that was clearly not lost on ancient man, who kept the animals close by.

Close Relatives of the Gray Wolf

This table shows all the members of the Order Carnivora including the Family Canidae (dogs, wild dogs, wolves, and jackals)—the same Order and Family as the gray wolf. Canis, lycaon, and cuon all possess 78 stable diploid chromosomes, a fact that allows these members of the family to interbreed and produce fertile offspring. Members who can interbreed are shown above the dotted line. Below the line we see other members, including foxes, of the *Canidae* family.

GENERA	SPECIES	COMMON NAME
Canis	Canis familiaris	Domestic dog
	Canis adustus	Side-striped jackal
	Canis aureus	Golden jackal
	Canis mesomelus	Black-backed jackal
	Canis simensis	Ethiopian wolf
	Canis lupus	Gray wolf
	Canis rufus	Red wolf
	Canis latrans	Coyote
	Canis familiaris dingo	Dingo
Lycaon	Lycaon pictus	African wild dog
Cuon	Cuon alpinus	Dhole
Nyctereutes	Nyctereutes procyonoides	Raccoon dog
Fennecus	Fennecus zerda	Fennec fox
Vulpes	Vulpes chama	Cape fox
	Vulpes velox	Swift fox
	Vulpes macrotis	Kit fox
	Vulpes vulpes	Red fox
	Vulpes cana	Blanford's fox
	Vulpes pallida	Pale fox
	Vulpes rueppelli	Ruppell's fox
	Vulpes benglensis	Bengal fox
	Vulpes corsac	Corsac fox
	Vulpes ferrilata	Tibetan sand fox
Chrysocyon	Chrysocyon brachyurus	Maned wolf
Cerdocyon	Cerdocyon thous	Crab-eating zorro
Dusicyon	Dusicyon culpaeus	Culpeo
	Dusicyon griseus	Gray zorro
	Dusicyon gymnocerus	Azara's zorro
	Dusicyon microtis	Small-eared zorro
	Dusicyon sechurae aka Pseudalopex sechurae	Sechuran zorro
	Dusicyon vetulus aka Pseudatopex vetulus	Hoary zorro
Speothos	Speothos venaticus	Bush dog
Urocyon	Urocyon cinereoargenteus	Gray fox
	Urocyon littoralis	Island Gray fox
Alopex	Alopex lagopus	Arctic fox

Living Together

However, waste disposal was not the only advantage to be gained from coexisting with the wolf. Wolves were skilled and successful predators at a time when the hominids' hunting skills were still primitive. Even the world's supreme predator, the tiger, is successful only on an average of one attack in ten. The hominids' strike rate was no doubt much less than this and it would have been well worth their while to follow the wolves in order to scavenge their leftovers. This is a custom rural inhabitants of the Indian subcontinent have always adhered to with abandoned tiger-kills, which are often large and extremely tasty deer.

Early man may also consciously have copied some of the successful wolf's hunting tactics. In Wyoming, once dominated by prairie grass, the wolves lay down and waved their tails to attract shy but curious antelope close enough to be killed; Shoshoni Indians use the same ploy to trap their dinner, merely substituting a strip of hide for a tail. Both wolves and American Indians drive large animals on to ice, where they lose their footing and become easy prey.

Learning from the Jackal

In contemporary times the first glimmerings of the process of domestication may be seen in another canid, the golden (or Asiatic) jackal. Keoladeo National Park in Bharatpur, Rajasthan, is home to as many as a thousand of these intelligent creatures, but increasingly, times are hard for wildlife. Droughts occur sometimes, as happened in 2001 for the third year in a row, and an ever-burgeoning human population means that cattle are taken into national parks where they compete with wild herbivores for food, depriving carnivorous predators of their prey species. Some of these golden jackals, like the wolves before them, are capitalizing on the advantages of lurking near friendly human habitation, in this case the Hanuman, or monkey-god, temple on the fringes of the forest. The temple is a little ramshackle, the walls of its courtyard cracked and in disrepair, leaving it conveniently open to nature. Monkeys chatter on its corrugated iron roof while colorful birds sing in the trees, but as dusk falls these creatures become

In Bharatpur, Rajasthan, jackals have taken to lurking near human habitation to find food, including in the environs of ancient temples.

A jackal waits in the dusky night for the call of the temple Baba.

silent and the creatures of the night begin to stir. It is now that Baba, the temple priest, sits in his courtyard calling to the jackals with a high-pitched cry. It may take thirty minutes or even longer for the first jackal to appear, timidly putting its muzzle through a crack in the wall. Baba continues to call while throwing the jackal a scrap, which normally occasions it to run back to the safety of the *ghana*, but very slowly the jackals gain confidence and finally venture into the courtyard and gobble down the scraps. But no tidbit is succulent enough to induce the jackals to come nearer than ten feet (approximately three and a half meters) to a human, and the slightest movement causes them to melt into the darkness of the forest.

Losing the Fear of Man

Hundreds of thousands of years of physical proximity and ever-increasing familiarity between wolf and human led finally to a close and interdependent relationship, not because the wolf's essential wild nature changed, but because over the generations a kind of natural selection occurred. The wolves who were least frightened of humankind were naturally the wolves bold enough to enter the fringes of human encampments. Interbreeding between these, braver wolves very slowly altered the levels of neuro-transmitters such as serotonin, and hormones such as adrenaline in generations of their offspring, which meant that, along with other wild characteristics, they lost their fear of man altogether.

Behavior modification as radical as this brought with it many morphological, or physical, changes which can be seen in exaggerated form in today's pet dogs: Dwarfs—miniature dachshunds; giants—Great Danes; wavy and curly hair—water spaniels; curly tails—Basenjis; floppy ears—Afghans. These are traits not usually seen in the wild and have resulted from the interbreeding of tame animals. Confirmation of this theory has been demonstrated by Belyaev and Trut in Russia in their transformation from wild to tame of another member of the dog family, the beautiful and curious silver fox.

Learning from the Fox

Taken from incarceration in Russian fur farms, Belyaev and Trut selectively bred silver foxes exclusively for tameness. Only cubs that on sexual maturity showed some affection toward their handlers, such as wagging their tails, were allowed to procreate and produce the following generation. In the beginning the overwhelming majority of the wild foxes either fled from their handlers, bit them, or, when stroked or handled, resolutely ignored them. However, after just six generations of breeding for tiny forms of affection, foxes were being born that were actively interested in communicating with people. They whimpered, sniffed their handlers, and licked them with enthusiasm. By the tenth generation these tame foxes represented 18 percent of the population; by the twentieth, 35 percent; and finally, after forty years and thirty-five generations, 70–80 percent. Such was these foxes affection for humans that, when some escaped, they turned their backs on their natural habitat and returned "home." Docile and friendly just like pet dogs, they competed with one another for human attention.

A domestic fox returns home from a stroll with a companion in Siberia.

Over the years Trut and others have raised these tame foxes at home as pets. Trut says of them: "They have shown themselves to be good-tempered creatures, as devoted as dogs, but as independent as cats, and capable of forming deep-rooted pair bonds with human beings—mutual bonds as those of us who work with them know." Although not identical to dogs (foxes start off with a slightly different genome), Trut believes they could be just as rewarding as pets. She says: "If fox pups could be raised and trained the way dog puppies are now, there is no telling what sort of animal they might one day become."

Obviously the transformation of wild wolf to domestic dog took tens of thousands years because the natural selection process was much less intense than that with Trut's foxes, but the neuro-chemical and neuro-hormonal changes that produced tameness in the fox and the wolf are similar. For example, over the generations, as the foxes became more tame, their adrenal glands' hormone production fell until after thirty generations it was just 25 percent of that of a wild fox.

Changes in the chemical make-up of the dog, after millions of years of domestication, mean that emotionally adult dogs carry the traits of their puppyhood.

An animal or human produces adrenaline when it is stressed, so this drop in its production meant that, unlike wild foxes, Trut's foxes were not stressed by human contact. Conversely they also produced much more serotonin than their wild relatives, which inhibited aggression. Their mating season lengthened—some bred out of season, some twice a year but, to date, no offspring have survived from this second mating. All these neuro-chemical and hormonal changes mean that in tame foxes, and dogs (as tame wolves are known) the emotional traits of cub- and puppyhood fail to disappear at maturity, as they would in wild animals, but endure for life.

Dog breeds illustrated in Leclerc De Buffon's *Histoire Naturelle*.

Many people believe they can tame a top predator such as a wolf and that this "tame" animal will feel affection for them. This is fantasy: wild predators, even crosses, behave in a tame manner only out of need or fear. During the eighteenth century exotic menageries were *de rigueur* for the wealthy and many aristocrats took a great interest in natural history. A not infrequent experiment was to cross wolves with domestic dogs. M. le marquis de Spontin was generous enough to give some such crosses to the greatest French naturalist of the time, Leclerc De Buffon. Writing in his seminal work *Histoire Naturelle* with great perspicacity, Buffon explains that the nature of these crosses was such that if the creatures were given their freedom they would immediately revert to wild ways, and writes that although once he recognized the man who brought him meat he would lick his hands and face, he did this only out of need. The animals attacked all others who approached them.

William Philadelphia, a noted big-cat trainer in the early twentieth century, explains with outstanding clarity the mechanism behind the "tame" behavior of wild animals:

"The wild beast is afraid, not so much of any pain that may be inflicted upon him, but of some vague unknown power too great for him to understand or cope with. This is what gives the tamer control of his lions and tigers. It is not any personal magnetism or any inherent virtue not possessed by other men—it is merely that one particular man, by untiring patience has succeeded in making himself appear in the lion's eye as the one great and boundless force of the universe before which he must bow."

Wolves, like big cats, can be trained but never tamed. In fact some might say that it is both cruel and irresponsible to want a top predator as a pet. In a domestic environment they are constantly anxious, being unable to exercise their natural desire to flee from humans and to kill for their food. They are intelligent animals placed in situations that bore and frustrate them. And, as a result of this boredom and frustration, many animals may even attack the person who apparently (in our human eyes) seems to be taking care of them.

As well as the hormonal and chemical changes, Trut's tame foxes underwent morphological transformations—just as did wolves as they became dogs. The color of the foxes' coats began to change, and some developed areas of white fur, often in the form of stars on their heads, something frequently seen in dogs and domestic horses. A few generations later fox cubs with floppy ears or curly tails were born. After twenty generations shorter legs and tails became evident; and by 1991 even the shape of the foxes' skulls was altering, a phenomenon which is very noticeable in tame wolves.

Early signs of domestication include the appearance of piebald coloring.

When Did Wolf Morph into Dog?

MtDNA, which showed us that the wolf and the dog are one (see p.8), undergoes mutations in its makeup at relatively constant time intervals. By comparing the number of mutations in the mtDNA of 162 wolves in 27 different geographical areas with that of 140 dogs from 67 different breeds, Robert Wayne (from UCLA) was able to estimate that the true tame wolf—or pet dog—first appeared on earth one hundred thousand years ago.

Archeology, however, tells a different story. Remains unearthed in Central Europe may date back 17,000 years, but the first undisputed canid—his short jaws and crowded teeth distinguishing him from the wolf—is a mere 14,000 years old and was discovered in the Near East.

So what of the 85,000 years in between? Could it be that ancient dog fossils exist but have yet to be discovered, or is it that for tens of thousands of years the domestic dog retained the morphology or shape of the gray wolf, but its phenotype, or behavior changed; in short it was a pet in wolf's clothing.

GRAY WOLF
The gray wolf is the direct ancestor of all modern pet dogs.

short, pricked ears

powerful jaw

two-layered coat

pads withstand extreme cold

DALMATION
A dalmation shows several of the domestic character-istics of the pet dog.

droopy ears reduce communication rang

flattened muzzle: les than half th wolf's crus ing power

piebald coat

Skeletal changes were among the last to occur in Trut's tame foxes (see pp.13–15) and no doubt this would have been the same for wolves. Although the wolf populations that lived on the fringes of human encampments would have formed their own packs, facilitating the development of a gene pool, which would in time turn the wolf into the domestic dog, there would always have been sporadic out-breeding. This would have added to their genetic diversity and slowed down the development of the more extreme morphological changes.

It is perhaps no coincidence that the period during which man began to abandon a hunter–gatherer's lifestyle for that of a farmer is also the period from which the first domestic dog remains date. An agrarian culture would have made quite different demands on the tame wolf. Humans would have found specialist activities, such as herding and guarding, increasingly desirable. In addition the all-too-human desire for a friendly furry companion would have asserted itself, leading humans to select and breed tame wolves with these embryonic qualities. Of course, the morphological changes of domestication, such as curly tails and diminutive stature, would also have appealed to these early settlers, who would have begun to breed for looks they found appealing, fixing and amplifying these early changes.

Instinctively, early farmers would have begun to breed the first domestic dogs, not only for their ability to help with human work, but for their friendly behavior toward humans and looks they found appealing.

The Saluki

Perhaps the earliest purebred dog is the Arabic Saluki, a sight hound who follows the lightning-quick gazelle by sight, not smell. She hunts in tandem with her master, galloping alongside his horse, ceaselessly scanning the desert terrain until they sight their quarry, or in scrubland taking her cue from a hawk trained to locate gazelles from his vantage point in the wide blue, hot skies. Once the gazelle is in its sight, the Saluki, running at speeds of up to forty miles an hour (65km/h) brings down her prey—dinner, not only for her master, but also for the tribe and herself.

The Saluki's exact origins are shrouded in mystery, although the Arabs, who prized the Saluki above all creatures—they were cared for with the children when puppies; placed on camel-back when the nomads moved camp; fed them succulent female goat's flesh, camel and sheep's milk thickened with couscous, and luscious sweet dates; and decorated them with colored beads and amulets to ward off the evil eye—claim her for their own. She was first bred in the long-vanished town of Saluki, southern Arabia, and it was they who first introduced the Saluki to Egypt. What is certain is that the first image of a Saluki dates back to somewhere between 4400 and 4000BC, engraved on ceremonial objects of green slate which were discovered at Hierakonopolis (modern Gebelen) in Egypt. From that time on the Saluki and other types of prototype sight hounds consistently appeared in tomb decoration. The renowned Egyptologist Howard Carter, writing in *Cassell's Magazine* c.1929 noted: "They [dogs] are pictured on the

First Breeds in China

Seven thousand years ago the Chinese were already breeding dogs specifically to eat, which eventually led to the development of the extremely meaty Chow. By 3000BC the diminutive Pekingese had achieved cult status in the imperial court. The Emperor kept a "dog book" in which outstanding artists painted portraits of the most desirable Pekes, thereby establishing breed standards—a device much beloved of kennel clubs in the UK and US.

rock-cut tombs of Beni-Hassan [c.2000BC] with pricked ears (which some of the hounds imported [to England] after the First World War had, as a result of being cropped by their Arab breeders) which identifies them with the Saluki. The hounds were essentially sporting dogs of graceful form, the very embodiment of aristocratic bearing, with feathered drooping ears, feathered tails and quarters, flexible loins, a deep chest, and long lithe limbs admirably adapted for the chase."

Another specialist profession for Egyptian dogs was police work. Policeman Kay (Middle Kingdom, 2040–1782BC) patrolled the Western Desert in search of fugitives, assisted by his five faithful dogs. He is pictured on his tomb slab with two of the dogs standing beside him and three shown beneath him.

Paintings from the tombs at Beni-Hassan show the huge variety of domestic canines already in existence in Egypt in 2000BC.

Ancient Rome and Beyond

By ancient Roman times dog breeds had become somewhat more specific, but were essentially classified by their function, not their looks.

Pliny in his *Natural History* (*c.*AD77) identified seven types of dog: *bellicosi* and *pugnaces*—war dogs (divisions of fierce fighting dogs patrolled the empire's furthermost borders); *nares sagaces*—scent hounds; *pastorales pecuari*—sheep dogs; *pedibus celeres*—sight hounds; *venatici*—sporting dogs; and *villactici*—pets, or guard dogs. However, being a dog in Rome wasn't all fun, for Pliny reports that suckling puppies were thought such pure meat that they were sacrificed and offered to the gods.

The Romans had many much-loved lapdogs, as mournful epitaphs attest.

By 1551 the Swiss naturalist Conrad Gesner is able to expand on Pliny's classifications. Some of his types are the Maltese; Pet Dogs; Dogs used for Hunting Large Animals; Dogs that Hunt by Scent; The Swift Dog; Bird Dogs; Hybrids; Companion Dogs; Fighting Dogs; Shepherd's Dogs; House Dogs; and those who Guard Temples. John Caius, an English physician and dog aficionado writing in 1576, also describes such wondrous "dogges" as the Daunser, also known as Salator or Tympanista, who "daunce in measure at the musicall sounde of an instrument, as, at the just stroke of the drombe, at the sweet accent of the Cyterne, & tuned strings of the harmonious Harpe shoeing many pretty trickes by the gesture of their bodies. As to stand bolte uptight, to lye flat upon the grounde, to turn round as a ringe holding their tailes in their teeth, to begge for theyr meate and sundry such properties, which they learne of theyr vagabunicall masters." He also describes the Mooner, or *Canis Lunarius*, who "doth nothing but watch and warde at an ynche, wasting the wearisome night season without slombering or sleeping, bawing & wawing at the Moone a qualitie in mine opinion straunge to consider."

By 1800 the section on *Le Chien* in Leclerc De Buffon's *Histoire Naturelle* (see p.14) has drawings of 32 different breeds, with very detailed physical specifications comprising up to 36 different measurements including the size of the eyes, the length of the ears, and the circumference of the tip of the muzzle. Buffon includes two illustrations of basset hounds, one of which is already exhibiting the twisted legs that come from inbreeding. In the main, however, when compared with a contemporary breed-member, the physical qualities that identify it as a basset are nowhere near as extreme. Until breed clubs developed in the late-nineteenth century, with the exception of dogs such as the Pekingese, the Saluki, and the hairless Mexican Xolo, most "breeds" of dogs, such as pointers and retrievers, were actually the products of rather random crossbreeding and outbreeding, and varied considerably in looks and character. At the Cremorne Dog Show of 1863, the first large dog show ever to be held in England, there were 28 classes of dogs, comprising around one hundred different breeds. The homogeneity of each breed may be deduced from this excerpt of *The Field*'s report on the show:

The first large dog show in England was held at Cremorne in 1863. There was some concern over the authenticity of the winners in the St. Bernard class (see quotation, left).

"The first and second prizes in the Saint Bernard class were allotted to two very rough dogs, alike in other respects but not resembling the usual type of their class, being more like the Newfoundland except in colour. On the authority, we believe of Lord Garvagh, they were however pronounced to be 'the genuine article', and we have no right to dispute his decision, never having seen the dog on his native mountains."

Nowadays there are around four hundred pure breeds recognized by the American and British kennel clubs, all the result of selective breeding from the tame wolf. For the kennel clubs uniformity of appearance was, and is, all. Vital breeds such as Welsh Corgis were subdivided into Pembroke and Cardigan Corgis, the Pembroke having a shorter tail, somewhat shorter body and more pointed ears than the Cardigan, subtleties that would have been lost on earlier dog fanciers and which lead to ruthless inbreeding, often with disastrous results (see pp.32–6).

CHAPTER TWO:

WHAT YOUR DOG'S BREED MEANS

"Things that upset a terrier may pass virtually unnoticed by a Great Dane."

Dr. Smiley Blanton (20th century)

For thousands of years humankind has regarded the dog as a creature who, in many ways, is there to make life easier. Guards of home, children, and flock; herders; beasts of burden, sources of food and wool, retrievers and supreme hunters-without the dog, times for humans would have been harder and the progression to civilization and leisure time slow. For thousands of years we have bred dogs selectively. In this chapter we look at how successful communication with dogs requires an understanding of, and respect for, inherent breed characteristics.

Although there have always been pets, and a few ancient breeds, such as the Roman Empire's ladies' spoilt darling, the Maltese, were kept as professional companions, this was not the primary function of dogs.

Canines are extraordinarily adaptable: No other creature tries so hard to fit into our world, to do our bidding, but hundreds, even thousands of years of selective breeding, mean that a canine's basic desire to herd, guard, hunt, and retrieve is not just going to disappear. Sadly in a domestic environment these instinctive qualities can take on a very different guise. For example, guard dogs, bred to protect property, can become globally aggressive and take to challenging their owners—very undesirable if you are a Manhattan apartment-dwelling old lady. Furthermore, dogs bred to alert humans to danger by barking, finding wolves, bears, or even burglars in short supply, frequently bark constantly at nothing.

The qualities which, from our point of view, make pet dogs disagreeable are aggression and dominance toward us (especially children) or other canines; being territorial and over-possessive (of their owners, their toys, and most other things); physical excitability; barking; and, just as crucially, a lack of playfulness, friendliness, and natural affection—qualities that canine organizations and many books on choosing a pet dog tend not to address. Instead they give innocuous descriptions of breeds, such as "alert, loyal, and patient" (which really don't tell us very much at all). This means that instead of picking dogs for their characters and the way they behave, we all-too-often pick them because they are irresistible balls of soft fur, or because they have a charming snub nose or striking blue eyes; but cuteness, after all, is only fur deep.

Hart and Hart, US animal behaviorists who during the 1980's undertook extensive work into canine genetics, were determined to discover if there really were breed differences and that some canine characteristics were inherited, such as the tendency to bark, rather than social. Using the American Kennel Club's (AKC's) 55 most popular dogs, as well as the much-loved Australian cattle dog, Hart and Hart looked at thirteen vital canine qualities ranging from obedience to destructiveness. The researchers confirmed that many purebred dogs have distinct characteristics that no amount of training or visits to behaviorists will alter. However, by taking some time to understand your dog's natural heritage, and to discover what behavior you can expect from her (particularly in an urban environment), you can work around any perceived downsides and enrich and deepen your relationship one-hundred-fold. So, with Hart and Hart's discoveries in mind, let's look at a few breeds in more depth.

Children need a good-tempered, patient dog, such as a labrador.

Hart and Hart's Discoveries

Hart & Hart's results were fascinating. Least likely to snap at children were the trusty golden retriever and the ever-beloved labrador retriever, both selected for a mouth and bite so gentle they do not damage delicate game birds; followed by every child's dream the Newfoundland, in at number four, the blood hound; the fifth most popular dog was the basset hound and, at number six, the collie dog.

Yorkies—Yorkshire terriers—are often bought as children's companions, but this reputedly inoffensive and playful canine's silky lap-dog good looks conceal its professional status as rat killer, which accounts for its position as the second most likely dog to bite, eclipsed only by the tiny Pomeranian. Other top contenders were Scottish and West Highland whites—vermin despatchers; miniature schnauzers—

ratters, and the extremely aloof but somewhat possessive chow chow. The dogs most likely to bring their owners into submission, particularly if male, were—fox terriers, Siberian huskies, Afghan hounds, miniature schnauzers, chow chows, and Scottish terriers—all, for different reasons, bred to be independent in thought and deed. Least likely to be a dominating influence was the ever-affectionate golden retriever. Hart & Hart also put dogs into different behavioral clusters. English bulldogs, Old English Sheep Dogs, Norwegian Elkhounds, Bloodhounds, and Bassets were ideal for people who want a placid dog around the house, as well as one who is not disposed to hassle other dogs while out on a walk. But these dogs' fatal flaw is they are not overly inclined to do our bidding.

Unchangeable Breed Characteristics

The Border Collie

Border collies are gorgeous. Their gloriously silky black-and-white fur, hypnotic eyes, bright intelligence, playful natures, and affectionate ways make people long to own them as family pets. In 1576 Dr Johanne Caius, author of the earliest British treatise on dogs, describes what must surely have been a dog very similar to the Border collie as follows: "The doggie either at the hearing of his master's voice, or at the wagging and whisteling of his fist, or at his shrill horse hissing, bringest the wandering weathers and straying sheepe into the self same place will and wishes is to have them …" The dogs have been bred selectively ever since.

The Border Collie

Collies are natural herders and have been used to herd sheep for hundreds of years.

A Happy Collie Must Herd

The American writer Jon Katz thought he had serious behavioral issues with his two-year-old Border collie until one day he realized that Devon was not misbehaving—but herding. Armed with this realization Katz and Devon, together, learned how to herd sheep. They now practice three or four times a week, and Devon is no longer a "problem" dog.

In the US there are several ranches where urbanites can allow their herders to do what comes naturally. Ted Ondrak, who runs one of these ranches, commented to the *LA Times*, "Most people are amazed to learn that the breeds they own are herding breeds. Those who love their dogs are happiest doing what makes the dog happy. And if you see the dogs' faces when they start herding, you know beyond the shadow of a doubt they love it. That's what makes it so magical."

For a Border collie, herding is its own reward: It isn't dependent upon treats or training, and she loves it the way a professional skier loves taking a crisp, white slope at 30mph—and this is never going to change. After twenty years of studying Border collies, scientists at Hampshire College in the US state quite unequivocally that it is simply impossible to train these dogs to do anything else and that, essentially, the same goes for all specialist dogs. As they further elucidate, "hounds often do very well as racing sled dogs, but their drivers are in perpetual fear of crossing a game trail and having the chase instinct elicited. Leaving the groomed track with 16 dogs in pursuit of a rabbit can be an exciting moment in the life of a driver."

Desperate to herd, Border collies will shepherd you back from the bathroom at Starbucks, bolt after next door's valuable Siamese and keep it penned on the window ledge, speed after you—and the bus, and, as a last resort, run maniacally around the house hoping that something will move. Coppinger and Coppinger in their article "Differences in the Behavior of Dog Breeds" cite that one AKC-registered collie "was reported as having a psychological stereotypic disorder causing it to fixate on an imaginary moving dust particle, followed by a forefoot stab. The therapists/vets were treating it with tranquilizers. In this case it was merely displaying a working motor pattern which has taken herdsman a century to perfect, and which is being displayed by a genetically well-bred, but bored household pet." It is not acceptable to tranquilize a dog. The vet, like the caretaker, had not taken the collie's natural characteristics into account.

As is so frequently the case with a purebred pet and its human companion, it was not the dog that was the problem, it was the environment in which it lived. Border collies are intelligent, agile dogs who become bored, frustrated, and drive their caretakers mad if expected to do nothing but lounge at home all day. But exercise by itself only creates only an insatiable athlete—collies need body and mind stretched. Herding three times a week is clearly ideal (see box, p.27), but some simply adore learning tricks, while others may find a vocation in frisbee.

Sheep Guards

Sheep guards would never indulge in disturbing, collie-like "eye, stalk, and chase behavior." Instead they are attentive, trustworthy, and defensive of their charges. Originally, guard puppies were raised with their sheep. During what scientists now term their "critical socialization period" their contact with humans was limited and those with any tendency to injure stock were swiftly removed (a practice Navaho Indians still adhere to with their small mongrels, who prove to be excellent guards). Over the centuries dogs bred from these sheep-socialized guards, such as Maremmas, have evolved into canines with virtually no predatory urges. The sheep are their friends—Maremmas often lick their charges' faces affectionately—and chasing has been so radically suppressed that many pets will decline to chase balls or play with toys. A disappointment for some children, but hardly a trait with serious consequences.

Maremmas often show great affection toward their charges.

Arctic Breeds

Like herders, Arctic breeds have very distinctive behaviors. Originally, this was because of the particular needs of tribal peoples, such as the Inuits; and over the last eighty years because Westerners have bred them specifically to pull sleds along groomed trails.

Who needs reindeer when there are Arctic breeds to pull sleds?

Sled and freight dogs are powerful, well-muscled, determined, supremely intelligent, and bred to survive in some of the most dangerous and tough conditions on the globe. As Benedict Allen, the explorer who attempted a solo sled crossing of the frozen Bering Strait between Siberia and Alaska, says, "they know the rules of the Arctic." Able to sniff open water (human and dog are dead once the sled goes in water), arctic dogs sense and drive off polar bears, and crucially take humankind where he could never venture alone. Allen's life was quite literally in their paws—and he felt humbled before their skills.

However, the dogs are also dependent upon their driver because if he fails to scout a proper route, or gets lost, the chances are they will all die. Knowing this, sled dogs do not give their trust lightly and will, to save themselves, desert a driver if they do not have faith in him. It was six weeks before Allen's lead dog would accept instructions to move left or right, but finally his team accepted him, and they judged him correctly.

Attempting to scout a route through jumbled pack ice alone, Allen became lost. Twenty-four long hours later, the explorer found his dogs waiting patiently for him and knew then that "they would go to the end of the world" for him. Feeling an intense loyalty to these animals and a genuine duty to ensure that every one of them returned safely to base, Allen "more or less then and there decided to turn around with them and go back." The Eskimo sled dogs of

The Samoyed-A Devoted Friend

Samoyeds traditionally moved and guarded the peoples' most important possession: their reindeer. Selected to bark at any sign of danger, be that bear or human, these dogs were kept in constant contact with the Samoyed people during the day, and slept in their tents at night, their glorious thick fur helping to keep their humans warm in temperatures of -40°F (-40°C). This level of socializing has given these dogs a profound love of people and an intense desire to talk (that is, bark) as a means of communication. These are traits that the dogs still possess today: they crave human company 24/7, are happier in a pack than alone, and will, regardless of what is or isn't out there, bark a great deal (far too much for any but the most tolerant of neighbors). Samoyed puppies are ideal pet-shop fodder—beautiful balls of fluffy white, cuddly fur, yours to have and to hold. But before you part with your money, think hard. Can you really spend all day, every day with her and tolerate her constant talking or is she going to turn out to be another "problem" dog?

THE SAMOYED

short set ears guard against frostbite

thick fur and underfur protect against arctic winds

broad back and deep chest gives endurance in harness

Admiral Edward Peary, an Arctic explorer of the early twentieth century, were less fortunate: "Day after day they struggled back across that awful frozen desert fighting for their lives and ours, day after day they worked until the last ounce of work was gone from them and then fell dead in their tracks without a sound...".

Clearly Arctic dogs are very special dogs—independent and brave, hardy and strong. However, although loving and friendly, they do not necessarily make ideal pets—they almost all have a tendency to explore, which means they can often go missing. The Alaskan Malamute, for example, a dog that was traditionally set free in summer to feast on plentiful hare and fox, still has the desire to hunt which is a problem in suburbia where the only available prey are cats and other dogs. (According to a spokesperson for the UK Rescue Society, if your Malamute does prey on other animals, it is impossible to train them out of it.) A sobering statistic reveals that in America alone around 15 million dogs are destroyed every year because their owners cannot cope with some kind of long-term behavior that they view as a problem.

Alaskan Malamute

Cosmetic Breeding and Its Problems

The gene pools of working dogs have remained tremendously diverse because it was vital, no matter what their profession, that they were healthy and vigorous. All that changed during the nineteenth century with the advent of the dog show when, instead of being bred for temperament or ability, dogs began to be bred for very precise visual characteristics.

"Human nature being what it is, judges couldn't help rewarding dogs who appealed to their personal preferences for a certain coat colour or texture, slightly larger or smaller builds, the point of a nose or the curve of a tail. When such dogs garnered top honours, fanciers revised or scrapped their written standards, and purged their kennels of 'old fashioned' animals. The gene pools for each breed were sharply curtailed ... in an attempt to 'fix' the same cosmetic feature in their own stock."
Elizabeth M. Thurston, *The Lost History of the Canine Race* (1997)

The British Kennel Club was established in 1873, its American equivalent in 1884. Stringent cosmetic breed standards were fixed and qualification as a pure breed was limited to dogs whose parents had both been previously registered as that breed which has eroded genetic diversity in the dogs and prevented any meaningful outbreeding.

Genetic Inbreeding

One of humanity's most powerful taboos is incest, with particular revulsion arising on that between parent and child, and between siblings. Although there are clear ethical considerations involved, maintaining this taboo ensures a rich and diverse gene pool. Incest reduces the heterogeneity or variety of available genes and means that descendants are much more likely to suffer from genetic disorders. Repeated down through generations, this tendency increases exponentially until eventually it becomes more or less a certainty.

So, incest is taboo for humans and yet some contemporary breeders can find it acceptable in their dogs and mate daughter with father, mother with son, and brother with sister to maintain what they term as "breed purity." The result has been to bring into existence genetically compromised animals—which means that many of these dogs are destined for a life of pain.

The problem is that chromosomes (which hold our genetic make-up) come in matched pairs, one from each parent. Many of the genes in these chromosomes occur in variant forms, known scientifically as alleles. One allele will usually be dominant (that is, its quality will be expressed); the other, recessive (which means its particular quality or characteristic will be hidden if matched with a dominant allele). (See box, p.34.)

If a breeder finds it desirable for cosmetic breed purity to eliminate black fur, he will breed a white (ww) dog with another white (ww) dog. As black fur is dominant, no white dog can possess the black (B) allele and black fur is completely eradicated from the blood line. Although the breeder was interested in selecting for only this one characteristic, he will have also eliminated other dominant genes from the pool, allowing instead the expression of the qualities of other recessive genes. In a large gene pool the combination of two recessive genes would be infrequent, but in a limited pool it may occur in almost every member of that blood line.

Many recessive genes, or combinations of these genes, cause major

Understanding Chromosomes

Chromosomes are made up of pairs of dominant, recessive, or dominant and recessive alleles. The pairing will determine certain characteristics, traits, or qualities in the animal (be it human or dog). Take the simple example of a dog with black fur. Black fur is dominant over white fur (the allele for black fur is dominant and the allele for white fur is recessive).

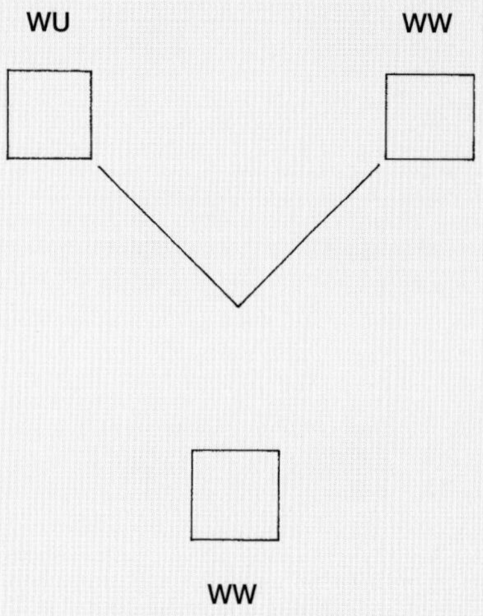

In the diagram shown below, BB denotes a dog with only dominant, black alleles (a black dog); WW denotes a dog with only recessive, white alleles (a white dog). The result of mating a BB dog with a WW dog can produce only a dog with black fur, because in each pairing the B allele dominates over the recessive W allele.

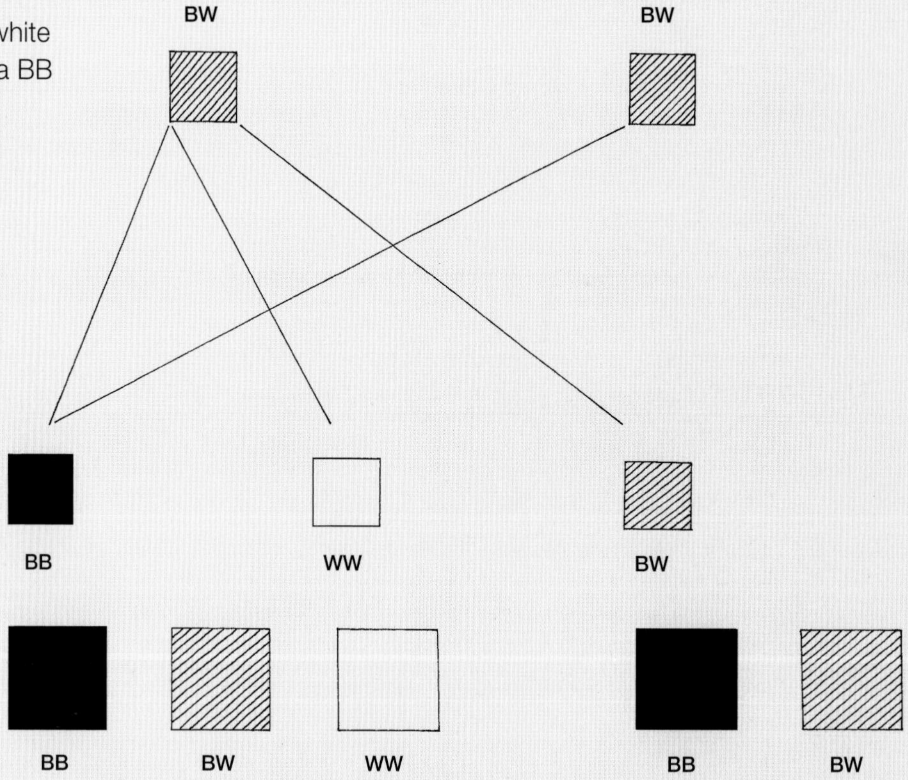

WU

WW

WW

BW

BW

BB

WW

BW

BB

BW

WW

BB

BW

Each year thousands of dogs compete at shows across the globe, which has led to a narrowing of the gene pool for dogs. Mongrels are likely to be genetically sound, with bright eyes, good teeth, and lively and intelligent natures.

physical disabilities and even mental health problems. This means that the majority of purebred dogs now suffer from genetic diseases, such as hip dysplasia (a condition in which the ball of the hip does not fit correctly into the socket) and progressive blindness. Tiny gene pools also lead to an overall loss of vigor in dogs and an average sixty percent mortality rate in litters.

Large sums of money ride on producing a champion and sadly this is likely to dampen any major efforts at outbreeding just in case the dog's physical appearance ceases to conform with show standards. The AKC disqualifies Bernese Mountain dogs if they have blue eyes; Siberian husky bitches if they are over 23$^1/_2$ inches (approximately 60cm) tall; Akitas if they lack pigmentation on their nose—and so the list continues.

But many dogs, directly as a result of inbreeding, suffer pain and disability. You could say that their plight is little different from those dogs bred for disease or physical deformity (this occurs in order to "further" medical science)—but at least these dogs have organizations working to ban experimentation on animals. Who champions the purebred?

Face Lifts for Dogs?

In the West cosmetic surgery is almost the norm because it is the visual which is used to signal status, power, and character. It hardly then comes as a surprise that Supreme Crufts' Champion 2003, Yakee a Dangerous Liaison, a Pekingese known as Danny to his nearest and dearest, should be accused in the national and international press of having had a face lift (a charge strenuously denied by his owner.) The UK Kennel Club, in their press release, wrote, "Having thoroughly researched the matter and taken veterinary advice, the Kennel Club can now confirm that no breach of its regulations occurred. The dog had undergone surgery to alleviate an acquired respiratory tract condition but, as this procedure did not alter the natural conformation of the dog, 'permission to show' was not required from the Kennel Club."

Entropian in Purebreds

Entropian, a particularly miserable and painful hereditary eye condition in which dogs' eyelids curl inward, is now common in a great many breeds. It causes squinting, constantly watery eyes, and often sensitivity to light. Dogs rub their deformed eyelids and, in time, the constant irritation ulcerates and scars the cornea, impairing vision.

The UK and US show rings ban dogs who have had an operation to alleviate the problem on the grounds that this will prevent them from being bred from. (However, some kennel clubs I have spoken to do admit that it is common for breeders to try to hide entropian in their dogs and, such are the advances in ophthalmic surgery for dogs, that operations can be hard to detect, encouraging many breeders to show their dogs anyway.)

Common Problems for Purebreds

Many ordinary people buy purebred dogs because they adore the way they look—how gorgeous are those Dalmatian's spots? How butch yet full of oriental mystery is the Akita? How sublimely elegant is that sleek borzoi? Often, we have absolutely no idea of the genetic diseases from which a purebred dog is likely to suffer.

If you are thinking of buying a purebred, you should know that disreputable breeders have been known to conceal health issues in their particular breed of dog. For an unbiased and genuinely helpful resource, which details the diseases from which your preferred breed could suffer and gives the chances of her inheriting those diseases, visit the website of Canine Inherited Disorders at www.upei.ca./~cidd/ intro.htm. As a taster, and a warning to beware, here are two of the problems, in only two purebreds, that you may encounter: The Dachshund's back is now so long in comparison to her short legs that many Dachshunds suffer spinal damage and end their days trundling around on wheels; the bulldog has such a severely compromised respiratory system that she gasps perpetually for breath, while her pelvis is so deformed that she can give birth only by C-section.

US researchers Coppinger and Coppinger point the way forward: "Most working dog breeders merely breed the best with the best regardless of morphological or behavioral considerations. Perhaps the lesson for the household dog industry is that until we understand behavior genetics it would be advisable to breed the best companion dogs to the best companion dogs regardless of other considerations."

In Praise of Mongrels

London's famous Battersea Dog's Home used to be full of mongrels, mutts, curs, and crossbreeds, abandoned for being too low class. Now 95 percent of their dogs are purebreds, while mongrels, those bastions of genetic diversity, vigorous rude health, and good temperament, are becoming increasingly scarce.

And yet, for most people hankering after a canine companion, a mongrel's sterling qualities must surely place her near the top of the list. So, I could not conclude this chapter without giving over a few words in full praise of mongrels! She is intelligent and curious, has no specialist behavior traits to cause her owner to wring his hands in misery or send her to the pound. She is most likely genetically sound and will have a healthy respiratory system, clear eyes, white teeth, strong legs, and a puppy-bearing pelvis. Her immune system will be strong; her vet's bills low;
and she will love you with all the devotion of which a canine is capable. What more could anyone want?

CHAPTER THREE:

TRANSLATING DOG

"Children and dogs are as necessary to the welfare of the country as Wall Street and the railroads."

Harry S. Truman (1884–1972)

Dogs, as every canine caretaker knows, are aware and perceptive creatures with unique personalities-their expressions of love, joy, disappointment, and desire leaving no doubt that they emphatically inhabit the here-and-now. Mainstream science, and many other groups, have labored tirelessly to deny self-consciousness in dogs (and other creatures) and are particularly insistent that animals can't use language, have abstract thoughts, or feel emotions. Despite all that, this chapter is intended to show you how, with a little bit of practice, it is perfectly possible to open up channels of communication with your dog-to understand and to be understood.

One way in which the scientific community reinforces the view that dogs and other animals have no self-consciousness is by asking dogs, chimps, and so on to perform tasks that involve some peculiarly human characteristic, such as multiplying numbers. When the animals fail the results are used as evidence of the creatures' lack of intelligence.

Some researchers maintain that dogs lack intelligence by testing them using tasks involving human skills. How might humans fare if asked to undergo tests involving canine skills?

But to turn this around, imagine an alien race testing us, using peculiarly canine characteristics—such as the ability to sniff out those still living buried under tons of earthquake rubble. Humans are hopeless at this task—sniff as we might—but does this represent clear evidence of our lack of intelligence? Perhaps the aliens would decide to give us another chance to prove ourselves. They might take us out for a four-hour hike across unknown territory and then set us free, with neither map nor compass, to make it home. We would fail again and no doubt have to be rescued from the middle of a muddy field. We really are stupid, conclude the aliens—after all, these were such easy tasks that even a dog could do them.

These kinds of attitudes have seeped into everyday consciousness without our even realizing it. In dog training, for example, the emphasis has been not on communication and understanding, but on our winning a power struggle for dominance, making canines rigidly obey our orders. Given that most caretakers describe their dogs as their friends, this seems a curious state of affairs—surely a friendship is a relationship with much more give and take? In the past the training goal was often achieved by using physical cruelty, and even today there are people who feel it perfectly acceptable to use choke chains with inward-pointing spikes, and collars that deliver electric shocks, to make their dog do what they want. A popular training mantra is that we must control everything our dog does. This includes removing all her toys except one, and letting her play with that only when we say so; not letting her eat before we do; and not letting her cuddle up on the sofa, and even ignoring her if she places her head upon our knees hoping for a sign that she is loved—even affection must be given only when we say so and not when our dog, for whatever canine reason, feels the need for love and reassurance. The hapless dog is often denied all self-expression, is never allowed to take the initiative, and is thus utterly and entirely dependent upon her owner for every action—a condition that substantially alters canine behavior, making dogs *appear* stupid.

Dependent Dogs and Dependent Owners

The creation of intensely affectionate relationships between canines and their human companions also make for very dependent dogs.

In Hungary, researchers presented dogs from very loving homes as well as more independent dogs with a simple test. Tempting treats were put in plastic dishes tantalizingly just within reach of the dogs, but behind a wire fence. All the much-beloved canines had to do to make the treats theirs was to pull on the protruding handle of the dish and drag the treats under the fence to their side. The dependent canines were simply hopeless at the task. However, as soon as these seemingly "dumb" dogs were encouraged by their humans—if you like, given permission to be independent—they solved the problem in a trice.

Interestingly the researchers found the reverse to be true when it was people who were utterly dependent on the dog, as are the blind with their canine guides. Here, the closer the relationship, the more the dogs strove and succeeded in solving problems for their human friends. But, what is even more fascinating is that these canny canines stepped in only when their assistance was actually needed. Showing sensitivity, insight, and empathy, they demonstrated the ability to see into another's (moreover a human's) mind and to exercise judgment—often in a split second. To use a Guide Dogs for the Blind Inc. phrase, these dogs displayed "intelligent disobedience."

"If the dog can become its companion's eyes then the distance between what a human sees [and understands] and what a dog does cannot be that great."

Blind individuals' descriptions of their relationships with their guides hint of something unquantifiable and, for the sighted, perhaps unknowable in the depths of mutual consciousness. One said: "[This is] the kind of relationship that we will never have with a human being and it's not possible with human beings... People have often tried to find the human equivalent to the relationship I have with my dog, but there isn't one. People ask me if she's my best friend, or if she is more like my child. [My dog] is my eyes. What is the relationship with your eyes?" Another said "With a dog you are whole. You are not two people [note the word people here] trying to function together, you're one unit. Even though you are two bodies it doesn't feel that way."

In 1995, Link Hill, who can neither hear nor speak, fell into the raging waters of the Yuba river in California. Of course, Hill was unable to call for help, but Boo, his trusty Newfoundland, quickly and correctly assessed that his companion was in danger of drowning. In an amazing display of true judgment, the dog leaped into the water, and towed Hill to the shore.

The guide dogs and their humans together transcend the boundaries between the human animal and non-human animal minds, developing modes of communication and forming a magical and complex relationship, which—wonderfully—is open to us all.

Looking in the Mirror

Further purported evidence that dogs are not self-aware comes from their seeming inability to pass Gordon Gallup's mirror test, its premise being that only creatures who can recognize themselves in a mirror are self-aware. Recognizing our own image may prove self-consciousness, but is it necessarily so that being *unable* (if that is what it is) to recognize one's own image proves a lack of self-consciousness—and thus the inability to empathize, sympathize, and understand others' points of view? Even a few examples of guide-dog behavior prove not. Gallup, a scientist at State University New York, put sociable chimpanzees in cages with nothing for company but a full-length mirror for what must surely have been an interminable ten days. Initially the chimps tried to socialize with their mirror image but after a few days they started to use the mirror to groom themselves—in other words they recognized their own image. To prove his point Gallup then gave the chimps a general anesthetic in order to paint red marks on their foreheads. When they came round they showed no sign that they were aware of the mark but when put in a cage with a mirror, the chimps became extremely curious and touched the strange mark constantly. No dog-lover wants to place their canine in a cage for ten days to prove Gallup wrong, but you could try the modified version in the box below.

A Simple Mirror Test for your Dog

Try this modification of the Gallup test on your dog. You will need a large mirror and some bright, non-toxic children's play paint.

1. Place your dog in front of the mirror so that she can see her whole body. Do this for a few minutes every day for a couple of weeks.
2. Initially, sit with her so she can see your reflection, too. Note if she catches your eye in the mirror, and also any reaction she has to her own image, both when you are with her and when she is alone.
3. At the end of the two weeks, put a large dab of the paint on your dog's head. Obviously there is no need to give your dog a general anesthetic, but you might try applying the paint while she is sound asleep after a particularly long and tiring walk. After an hour or so, sit her in front of the mirror again. If she notices the paint—for example, by trying to rub it off with her paws—then your dog is a certified sensate genius.

Place a life-size painting or photograph of yourself in front of your dog to see how she reacts.

Dogs tend to ignore their own image. Humans and chimps, however, spend inordinate amounts of time grooming themselves, dogs do not; humans are extremely vain and it is not hard to imagine chimps also possess this trait. If it is not to groom or to admire their image, it is hard to imagine just why a dog would want to spend any time gazing at herself. But this doesn't mean that dogs don't understand what mirrors are. My canine friend Poppy has two methods of getting my attention while I groom myself, to use scientific speak. She either nudges me with her huge wet nose or catches my eye in the mirror (just as a human would). Common sense dictates that she must recognize that what she sees in the mirror is my image and not actually me, and thus understand that the dog in the mirror is herself. Many other dog caretakers report the same.

This anecdote (by Louisa Starr Canziani) from *The Spectator Book of Dog Stories* nicely illustrates a canny canine learning the difference between an image and reality, albeit in a different medium. Why not try it at home?

"Some time ago I was painting two portraits in the country, and one day by chance I placed the picture of my hostess on the ground. Immediately her old spaniel came and gazed intently at the face for several seconds. Then he smelt at the canvas, and unsatisfied, walked round and investigated the back. Finally having discovered the deception, he turned away in manifest disgust, and nothing we could do or say, on that day or any other, would induce that dog to look at the picture again. We then tried putting my portrait of his master also on the ground but he simply gave it a kind of casual contemptuous side glance and took no further notice of it. We attributed this not to any difference in the merits or demerits of the two portraits but, simply to the fact that the dog felt he had been deceived once, but was not to be so taken in again."

Understanding Your Language

The scientific community likes to maintain that only *Homo sapiens* uses and understands language. However, increasingly, research is proving this supposition to be wrong. Take Rico, a gorgeous, intelligent, much-loved Border collie, who, at the time of this display of linguistic prowess, had reached the ripe old age of ten. Since puppyhood Rico's humans had been teaching him the names of a huge variety of children's toys by showing him the toy, repeating its name a few times, and then giving it to him to play with.

His caretakers frequently entertained themselves and Rico by putting three or so of his toys in different places and then asking him to fetch one in particular—a feat he carried out with great accuracy. By the time Rico's human companions enthusiastically agreed to let researchers test his skills, Rico already knew the names of two hundreds toys. When children pick up a new word they immediately figure out just what it means. So, say Timmy, aged three, is asked to pick out a kangaroo, a creature he has never heard of before, from a group of otherwise familiar toys, he will automatically pick the unfamiliar item as he deduces that the new name must belong to the new toy. Rico does the same and still remembers the name of the new toy a month later. When asked to fetch a strange floppy white bunny from a group of otherwise familiar toys, Rico bounded into the adjacent room, tail aloft, and after giving the toys a good look over, came out with the bunny firmly gripped between his teeth—a feat he managed seventy percent of the time. A month later Rico could still pick out the bunny, and other toys he'd correctly identified fifty percent

Rico, a Border collie, has a vocabulary of over two hundred words.

of the time, even when they were with four more new toys as well as four of his familiar toys—just as three-year-old children do.

Of course the crucial point is that Rico understands that objects have specific names and remembers them, proving that this ability to recognize and label objects must have evolved earlier than, as well as independently of, the ability to actually speak. In other words, language is part of the mind's general facility for learning and memorizing and, therefore, not the exclusive province of humans.

Although the shapes of canines' mouths and tongues mean that they are never going to actually vocalize any human language, they can use different sounds to convey different messages. Stanley Coren's book, *How to Speak Dog*, describes Kentucky local "Brother John" who bred Kentucky bluetick hounds "so that they got a good nose and some smarts and the desire to hunt," but "so's they can tell you what they're smelling .... Now Zeke here, he's typical of my breeding. When he's onto a rabbit, he's got a kind of a 'yip yodel' sound. When he's onto a squirrel, its mostly 'yip' and when he's got a noseful of raccoon, it's mostly 'yodel.' When he's got the track of a bear he gives a sort of growl bark but not very loud. If he gets a whiff of a big cat, he gives a mostly high—almost squeaky bark .... Redbones [another Kentucky breed of hound with 'the music' as this skill is called] are different from blueticks, but they seem to know each other's words. I was out near Brownsville once and Stephen [man not canine] was chasing a big cat with Hamilton, you know that big redbone of his. Hamilton's sound when he's hunting cat is mostly like my dogs' sound when they're hunting deer, only much more excited and broken up. Zeke hears Hamilton and takes off in the direction of his sound, but he's giving that squeaky bark of his which says cat. Maybe dogs' got dialects or may be they just translate other dogs in their heads." He continued, "It could be that they just make it up as they go just to keep us humans confused."

These hounds point to intriguing possibilities in the domain of canine–human communication, but I'm just going to sit back and wait for one of you to teach your dog to speak. Poppy is too busy chasing squirrels to apply herself.

Some dogs are just too busy to talk to us.

Learning from Gazing

At Harvard, researchers have been investigating canines' ability to understand our non-verbal communication by variously gazing at, pointing to, tapping, and marking one of two boxes that contained a treat. Non-human primates were none the wiser for this display although in time they learned what the signals meant; for wolves brought up by humans it was very much a hit-and-miss affair; but puppies just a few weeks old understood immediately what the researcher was telling them and went straight to their reward.

This seems perfectly natural given that dogs frequently use gaze-direction to communicate their own needs or wishes. For example, if my dog Poppy whines at me and I reply by saying "show me," she will go to the kitchen and stare doggedly at her water bowl, which will prove to be empty; her food bowl if I have forgotten to give her dinner; or the refrigerator if she knows it is full of bones and hasn't had one for a while.

What is unexpected, at least for scientists, although probably not for canine aficionados, is that domestic dogs seem to have a very specific facility for understanding our language. When not snoring on the sofa, our canine friends spend an enormous amount of time gazing at us. This is partially because they are waiting hopefully for a sign that a walk is imminent or that an unexpected juicy bone is arriving; but more than that they are doing their level best to understand us by absorbing our body language, voice inflexions, and the meanings of our words, and through this to figure out the underlying rules of our pesky human behavior.

Over the millennia, while ostensibly selecting dogs for their working traits, we have also selected them for obedience, the capacity for forming deep and affectionate bonds, and the ability to understand and be understood by us—or, to use science speak, where canine–human social-cognitive skills are highly developed. Dog owners the world over have always insisted that their dogs understand every word they say, and finally science is catching up with them. So, is really meaningful interspecies communication more than just a dream? Many researchers, tantalizingly, are beginning to think it is. Dog-caretakers often utter the phase "if only she could talk." Perhaps with real dedication, and within the limits of her own morphology, she can.

If dogs could talk, who knows what they might get up to when we aren't watching?

Understanding Your Dog's Body Language and Behavior

Worthwhile and affectionate relationships are based on real and effective communication and, for the human half of canine–human relationships, that means, among many other things, carefully observing our pets' body language in diverse situations and learning what our own body language means to them.

Communicating by Smell

Although canines constantly use the world of smell to communicate with one another, leaving messages on lamp posts, trees, and the pavement, and taking in the aromas of one another's genital regions, apart from ramming their noses into our crotches from time to time, their communications with us rely mainly on the visual, supplemented with vocalization and touch—with one exception, sharing the intense perfume of fox feces, skunk scent, or garbage. Poppy often walks with a large and, to most other dogs but her, formidable Akita. Almost always during the course of her walks she rolls in a stinking muddy stream filled with rotting vegetation and emerges coated with viscous goo. She then hurls herself at the Akita, rubs her body against him so that he too has this glorious smell (an attention he accepts with good grace), willfully coats the Akita's companion's legs with no resistance, and finally shares the smell with me.

What does this mean? Some experts speculate that rolling in foul odors attracts interest from other dogs thus making for a jolly social life; English zoologist Desmond Morris thinks it may be a call to hunt. No one knows for sure, but it seems undeniable that sharing this canine perfume is a sign of affection, inclusion, or even love.

The Importance of Ear and Tails

The repertoire of canine body language includes a host of emotions conveyed by the most subtle nuances of ear and tail position, posture, eye-contact, the raising of fur, and general facial expression. The fur of a Pekingese, skin-folds of a Shar Pei, and skull-shape of a pug preclude any diversity of facial expression, putting these breeds at a considerable disadvantage when communicating, and making interpretation of their moods considerably more difficult. The pug is further disadvantaged when owners have half her naturally floppy ears removed to make them stand up. Canine domestication brought with it the spontaneous emergence of floppy ears, just as it did for the domesticated foxes in Siberia (see pp.13–15). Floppy ears move using exactly the same muscles as prick ears and their shape only marginally reduces ear language. However, when these ears are reduced, the result is an immobile ear, which nullifies the dog's signaling ability. This practice has been outlawed in the UK, but in the US owners routinely dock purebreds such as boxers and Dobermans. A subject of controversy in which the American Kennel Club is involved, there is now a bill aimed at eradicating this disfigurement in the US.

In some countries, including the US, dogs such as this Doberman have their tails removed and ears reduced as a matter of routine.

In his book *Dogs Never Lie About Love*, Jeffrey Masson, Canadian psychologist and prolific writer of books about animals, writes:

"Tails as we all know are subtle and marvelous carriers of meaning, but when I acquired my present family dog I was not prepared for the complexity of a dog's ears. The expressiveness of Sasha's ears is something to behold. She can say as much with her ears as we do with our mouths."

In addition to the removal of ears, US purebred owners also practice tail-cutting in more than fifty purebred dogs—something which is now illegal in the UK; and some unfortunates, such as the Boxer and Doberman, are often deprived of both full ears and tail.

Besides playing a vital role in communication, tails, particularly in large dog breeds, are important for balance, providing a counter weight when taking a sharp bend at speed; whirring round like a Catherine wheel when coming to a sudden stop; and acting as a tight-rope walker's balancing pole when pottering along narrow walls or cliff-top ledges.

The tail is an essential part of the dog's balance mechanism—never send your dog out without one.

Some of those who condone docking claim that it doesn't hurt puppies because they cry out only after their tails have been cut. However, this delay is actually because pain transmission at birth is sixty times slower than in adulthood and, to quote the British vet and author Bruce Fogle: "It hurts as much as it would hurt to twist off the smallest finger of human new born babies without anesthetic." Docking also causes health problems later in a dog's life. To again quote Bruce Fogle: "Docked boxer dogs in particular have a higher incidence of back pain than those with tails. A tail is built to wag at a healthy speed. The fast metronome motion of a stump places excessive strain on the lower back, causing inflammation and eventual arthritic changes in the back bones."

Telling Tails (Revealing Ears)

The tail's enormous importance in communication is underlined by the fact that in most wild canines the color of the tip contrasts to that of the shaft, making tail signals highly visible even over considerable distances. Unambiguous expression is vital for the smooth day-to-day running of wolf packs, because it confirms previously established relationships without wasting time in needless conflict and posturing, and as wolf-expert Schenkel writes, the tail is the "most dynamic" element of this expression.

Common sense tells us that it is going to be much more difficult to interpret any dog's intentions, moods, and feelings if she has cropped ears and just a tiny stump for a tail and that misunderstandings are bound to occur. For example, imagine a canine growling at you with a wrinkled-up nose and exposed teeth. If this is a confident, assertive dog merely looking for acknowledgment of her superior status in the park, her ears will be upright or slightly forward, her tail stiff and more-or-less horizontal. An aggressive but frightened canine will have the same wrinkled-up nose and exposed teeth but her ears will be held back and flattened against her head, and her tail will be drooping between her legs. In other words the ears (and the tail) in the two scenarios convey two very different messages.

I am unaware of any studies to validate, or indeed invalidate, the view that depriving dogs of these two modes of communication leads to increased inter-canine aggression, but it seems a logical conclusion to draw when signals of negotiation, accommodation, and general groveling are as open to misinterpretation as are those of confidence, friendship, assertion, anger, or fear. Of course, friendly overtures are just as likely to be misinterpreted or even not noticed at all (the obvious example is that both humans and other dogs might miss the distant friendly wagging of a stump).

Even intact tails are not all alike and, when interpreting their meaning, we must always relate the tail's present shape and position to its natural, relaxed position. The proud Akita, for example, holds her tail up and curled over her back; while the Maremma, a more wolf-like canine, holds hers down and gently sloping from the back of her legs. Dogs maintain this relaxed position when walking around with no particular place to go or making a cursory examination of smells. If these smells prove to be something extremely interesting, such as fox feces, the tail will start to wag excitedly—the Akita's round and round like a helicopter; the wolf-type dog's from side to side.

The scope of this book, and perhaps any book about dogs, makes it impossible to delineate the many combinations of body language that dogs use to communicate with one another, and with us. Above all it is impossible to give every variation of tail expression for every type of tail, but careful observation of your own dog's tail will soon allow you to understand what it is saying. You can be sure that any effort you do make to interpret your dog's special sign language will be repaid a hundred times over in love and trust.

Greeting a New Canine Friend

1. Do not stare or gaze directly at the dog (she will consider this a challenge); avert your eyes a little.
2. Resist the temptation to put your hand out, palm down, over the dog's head and instead lift your hand, palm open upward, toward the dog's nose and let her sniff your fingers.
3. If she doesn't move off, and very often, for their own inscrutable reasons, dogs may not, do stroke her under the chin or rub her chest.

Saying "Hello"

Dogs acknowledge their human companions in many different ways. If relaxing under the table after a hard day's walk, dogs often reply to requests for affection or demands to "come here" by thumping their tail on the ground.

When waking up and checking that you haven't sneaked out without them, they nudge you with a cold, wet nose when they find you. They love to rub your nose with theirs to let you know they care—just as you stroke them for the very same reason.

Saying hello to strangers often means wanting to gather some solid information about them. For dogs the most convenient way to do this is to push their nose straight in to the stranger's crotch. You might notice your dog does this after you have had a bath, perhaps to check that underneath the clinging perfume of bath oil, you are still the same, essential you.

If being butted in the crotch isn't every human's favorite way of being greeted then having a human stare open-eyed at them while lowering their hand right over their eyes to pat them on the head

The lazy hello

and neck is distinctly undesirable for dogs. Although they will tolerate this if they must—they know they are meant no harm—dogs generally move their heads around, trying to avoid this unwarranted intrusion. This is partly because large dogs, as well as the assertively frisky, will put a paw over a younger, smaller (and sometimes not-so-small) dog's neck, or the top of her back or head; partly because the human is obstructing the dog's field of vision; and partly because steadfast gazing, other than in a play situation, is considered a challenge.

Getting to Know Each Other

When two unacquainted canines spot one another in the near distance, fifty feet (approximately 15 meters) away or even more, a common canine reaction is to adopt a stand-off, with tails held horizontally and moderately stiff—a cautious, conservative approach which does not signal assertion, aggression, or overt friendliness. Sometimes tentative but wide tail-wagging may occur—this is a clear invitation to friendship. If the stand-off continues for more than a few minutes often one dog will bound to the other leading to tail-softening and enthusiastic wagging by both parties followed by an introduction of mutual genital sniffing. Where the dogs are of the opposite sex, time and time again I

If a dog is jumping up at you, putting a hand out palm down above her head, while staring at her, will stop her in her tracks.

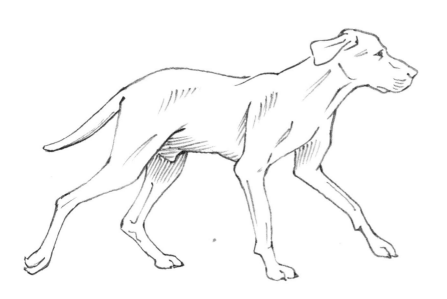

A tentative questioning approach, showing neither a request to romp nor any aggression.

Staging a Sit-in

Sitting down firmly is a way of neutralizing a boisterous or unwanted physical approach without the need for conflict. First, sitting means that the genital region is solidly planted on the earth denying the approaching dog detailed personal information; and second it gives the seated canine the opportunity to look around at the general environment as if unconcerned, hiding any admittance of inferior status, while the accosting dog vainly sniffs around her tail.

Although sometimes status driven, sitting down can also be a means of avoiding pain. An extremely arthritic dog of mine frequently did this as she got older because her joints were simply too painful to take the knocks of play or the strenuous movements involved in many rituals, or to run happily with pals through the woods. I have observed this behavior in many older dogs.

have seen one—and not necessarily the male—deposit a urine scent mark and the other examine this rich source of information carefully. Then, the second dog will deposit their own urine on top of the first dog's so that the first dog can smell this scent mark in detail before re-covering it with their own. The dogs will then go their separate ways. What this actually means is hard to estimate, but it is tempting to speculate that it is an agreement for cordial relations in the future, even sex. After all dogs, like humans, have their preferences. On other occasions, of course, one dog or the other may break the stand-off and bound happily off into the distance.

Sometimes approaches, whether from a stand-off or not, develop into rituals, which many behaviorists would describe in terms of dominance and submission. However, submission in these preeminently social situations may be no more than a desire to please—a request for friendship, albeit not one that the dog is certain will be granted. Note in particular the one raised paw and remember all the occasions that your dog has raised her paw to ask for a favor, whether it was opening a door or extracting her from a difficult situation.

The raised paw is a dog's way of saying "please."
Who could refuse such beautiful manners?

Being Pleased to See You

Dogs welcome back not only their companions, but other favorite humans, with great enthusiasm. They leap up to lick our hands or faces; they luxuriantly rub their sides against our legs; they wag their tails and bodies, and pant and run around excitedly.

You could call this submissive behavior—a dog tentatively approaching another will lick at its mouth or the air next to its face while wiggling her body to show inoffensiveness and acceptance of her lowly position—but surely this is an expression of delight and happiness, a genuine token of canine friendship; for those whom dogs dislike, they roundly ignore.

Twentieth-century novelist Elizabeth von Armin, in her autobiographical book *All the Dogs of My Life*, describes how her Swiss mountain dog first greeted her husband-to-be:

"he rushed to give him the welcome suitable to so important an arrival. He was in fact all over him. 'Come in, come in—oh, do come in! This is our house, but from now on it's yours and everything in it,' he seemed to be passionately conveying by leaps, licks, waggings, and loud, glad yelps."

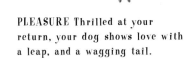

PLEASURE Thrilled at your return, your dog shows love with a leap, and a wagging tail.

55

Loyalty Beyond Measure

Hachinko was a faithful and devoted Akita, the long-term companion of Professor Eisaburo Uyeno in Japan. Hachinko accompanied the professor to Tokyo's Shibuya rail station every morning and waited there for him to return every evening. But one day the professor did not return: He had died at work. However, loyal Hachinko never gave up hope. He continued to visit the station every day for the next ten years, until finally he died at the very spot he last saw his human friend. Touched by Hachinko's fidelity, in 1934 Tokyo commuters erected a bronze statue of the dog inside the station. After the statue was melted down during the 1940's to help the war effort, The Society for Recreating the Hachinko Statue commissioned another as soon as peace was declared—which survives to this day.

Many dog trainers instruct canine caretakers to pay no particular attention to their dogs both when they leave them and when they return, in order to prevent excessive excitement in the dog. But how can your dog know if you will ever return? Who has not waited anxiously by a telephone for a lover to ring and been far too effusive when they finally called? And who has not waited in vain? I always imagine this is how dogs must feel when their companions are gone for more than an hour or two. Dogs can't go out for a walk to pass the time, visit a canine pal down the road, or crack open a beer. All they can do is wait for you.

When dogs are excessively excited before and when a caretaker returns home it is very often because they have been repeatedly left alone for long periods of time, and are desperately bored and frustrated. Desmond Morris addresses the problem succinctly in his book *Dogwatching*. He writes that dogs "are social beings and they are also intensely exploratory. If they are deprived of companions both canine and human—or if they are kept in a constrained or monotonous environment—they suffer. The worst mental punishment a dog can be given is to be kept alone in a tightly confined space where nothing varies."

Elizabeth von Armin (see previous page) was relieved that her dog liked her new husband.

No wonder "problem" dogs chew the furniture, rip up
the carpets, and attack the curtains—they are crying out for
stimulation. They don't need tranquilizers or behavior therapy,
they need companionship, exercise, and something to occupy
their alert and intelligent minds. Dogs chained alone in back
yards bark constantly. Canadian writer Jeffrey Masson suggests
that "they may simply be asking to be free." I agree with him.

Many years ago I adopted a rescue dog eighteen months old. She
howled desperately as if her very heart was breaking if left even for
a moment outside a store. I was sternly advised to continue to
tether her, walk into the store without concern, and ignore her
cries. Her howling became louder, longer, and if possible even
more desperate. After a few days of adhering to this "advice," I
changed tack. Instead, before I left my dog, I put myself on her
level and talked reassuringly to her for three or four minutes while
stroking her comfortingly. Then, when I entered the store, my dog
didn't howl—although she did look anxiously through the door
and begin to whine softly after a few minutes. As soon as I came
out I caressed her and comforted her again. After a week or so of
this reassurance she was perfectly happy to sit outside almost
anywhere. Like all dogs she had needed communication, not
a lack of it. She was able to give up her insecure behavior
through reassurance, rather than being finally forced to give
it up through lack of hope.

Certainly dogs who are not made any fuss of at all when their
companions return will soon learn not to express their delight, for
they need you to join in their joy too—if only for a minute.

Being Happy and Hopeful

Many dog trainers and behaviorists emphasize signals of dominance, submission, hierarchy, rank, and aggression, perhaps because they are so often presented with dogs whose behavior has become problematic for their human companions.

These terms have validity within their own constructs, but the canine world is not so simple and I believe that many canine relationships and rituals have their basis in bonding and mutual support, not hierarchy. Consequently, for many of us it is more relevant, rewarding, and ultimately useful to talk about signals of friendship, excitement, interest, anger, sadness, joy, loneliness, and trust; and the domestic dog's wonderful capacity for negotiation both with us and her fellow canine.

Dogs have so many ways of expressing joy, excitement, desire, and welcome. A companion wearing a pair of walking shoes can provoke a riot of dancing and whirling interspersed with play bows (see illustration, top left), as well as what many would describe as a submissive posture (see illustration, bottom left), but which is more an indication of trust in her companion and the hope of happiness to come. Tail-thumping, shining eyes, and galloping front legs represent an eloquent plea to accompany you wherever you may go, be it to the great outdoors or just round the corner to the local store. When you are sitting reading a book or watching the TV and your dog adopts this hopeful position, all the while looking at you out of the corner of her eye, she is asking for attention and affection, for her stomach to be

PLAY BOW This pose reveals an excited, playful dog, who may also whirl and leap in joy. Perhaps you have just indicated that you are about to go for a walk together.

TRUST This dog's submissive posture is actually more an indication of trust in her human companion.

rubbed, her chest to be tickled. Dogs love physical pleasure—take the example of the long hedge that lines my road for one hundred feet (30m). Conveniently trimmed to be twenty inches (50cm) above the pavement, it provides a wall of delightfully scratchy twigs and there isn't a dog in the neighborhood who doesn't rub its back on it—and emotionally it reaffirms their relationship with you.

Play bows in the park mean that your dog wants to play and the movement usually forms part of a whole series of bounds, chases, and mock attacks. In addition a dog will use play bows to nullify a previously over-assertive approach, whether she meant to be so forthright in the first instance or not. Once your dog has made a play bow there can be no misunderstanding: The message is "Hey! Let's play."

But perhaps your dog hasn't seen you wear your shoes—maybe you have merely walked past the front door and unconsciously looked at them because you are thinking of going out. Ever attentive, your canine will pick up on this slight cue and be wondering if something is going to happen. Most dogs will ask for a reply to this weighty matter quite clearly by sitting bolt upright, smiling,

A short privet hedge provides just the right place for unadulterated canine scratching.

EXPECTANCY Asking for a reply, your questioner sits bolt upright, smiling, and fixes you with their gaze.

ANTICIPATION Showing an expectant enquiry, the dog may cock its head to one side.

cocking their head on one side, and looking expectantly at their caretaker. Alert, interested, quizzical, and blinking slowly to let you know this enquiry is not a challenge, they will thump their tail on the ground as a sign of enthusiasm for any upcoming entertainment.

Why not reply? If I say the words "in a minute," Poppy knows a walk will happen soon and will whirl around with joy. If I say "yes" she will sit absolutely still next to the door gazing rigidly at the door handle. If I say "no" she will slink off to her bed, put her head between her paws and her ears back, and stare at me with disappointed, reproachful eyes (see illustration, below).

A less dire disappointment is shown by dogs lowering and pushing their heads forward while wagging their tails from side to side and looking into your eyes as if to say "Are you sure?" This body language also indicates a kind of sad hope when human companions have been preoccupied for what their dogs consider to be far, far too long, and they are hoping for, but not necessarily expecting, distraction—a bone, a walk in the park, or maybe a game of ball.

GRAVE DISAPPOINTMENT I thought we were going for a stroll? How can you disappoint me so?

The Tail as Barometer

As tails go up so does mood. A relaxed, broadly wagging tail indicates a cheerful dog, interested in everything around her. It is fascinating to watch the tail movements of a group of well-adjusted, off-leash dogs, walker in tow, rummaging through the grass, sniffing the breeze, and streaming through the woods. Their tails act as sensitive barometers of mood—the more fascinated or confident the dogs are at any given moment, the higher their tails rise and the more enthusiastic the wagging.

If a tail stops wagging, becomes horizontal, and stiffens a little, there is something unknown or worrying on the horizon. Closely observing how your dog's tail moves in different situations while you are both out walking will give you a wonderful insight into her moods and, even more than that, it may warn you of something or someone troublesome approaching.

Curled-tail dogs, such as Akitas, whirl their upright tails round and round rather like helicopter blades to express enthusiasm and friendly overtures.

As semi-upright and upright tails in wolf-like dogs become stiff they become princely symbols of confidence. Masters of all they survey, these dogs are not even considering the possibility of a challenge, but neither are they issuing one. If they wish to indicate being ready for a challenge, they raise their tail-fur.

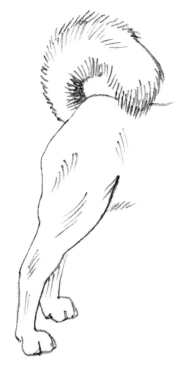

RELAXATION The normal position of an Akita's tail is with muscles relaxed and curled over her back.

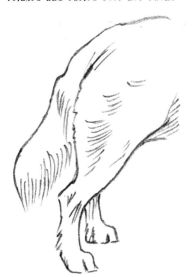

RELAXATION The tail position of a wolf-type dog: down and sloping gently away.

Aggression and Keeping the Peace

Wolves, and dogs, are great negotiators. Much of their body language is designed to prevent any outbreak of physical hostilities and it is only when negotiations have completely broken down, or two dogs of equal status want to make a point, that fighting will break out. Humans so often take submission in man and beast as an irresistible invitation to be unkind. Dogs almost never do (see box, opposite).

Wolves virtually never bite one another. To initiate biting is to invite being bitten, a counterproductive strategy unless a vital interest—such as, to quote author and conservationist Zimen: "In struggles for the alpha position in the pack, in driving rivals out of it or in clashes with wolves which were alien to it"—is at stake. Dogs are essentially no different. They have their own rules of engagement and it is almost always better to let them settle their own differences. Usually a "fight" will be no more than mutual teeth-baring and hearty growling accompanied by empty snaps in the air and, even if it progresses further, is unlikely to involve much more damage than perhaps a bitten ear before one dog humbly backs off. There are extremely occasional exceptions when the winner ignores the underdog's protestations of submission and surrender and instead moves in for the kill. If this happens the loser will let forth truly terrible and unmistakable screams. It is now essential to intervene.

Dogs will instinctively chase one another in circles.

Many caretakers, however, are excessively protective of their dogs to the canine's lifelong detriment. Their dogs, unable to practice

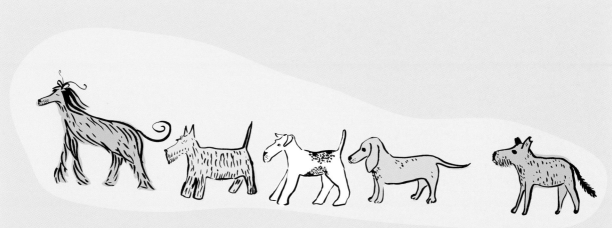

Belka, the Prison Dog

Fyodor Dostoevsky, the nineteenth-century Russian novelist, writing of his terrible time in prison, tells of Belka, a stray dog who had been run over by a cart and who was "all mangy, with suppurating eyes; his tail was almost denuded of hair and always carried between his legs. Thus abused by fate, he had plainly made up his mind to submit. He never growled or barked at anybody as though he did not dare. He lived for the most part behind the barracks, on scraps. If he ever saw one of us he would immediately, while we were still some paces distant, turn over on his back in token submission, as if to say, 'Do what you please with me; you can see I will not even think of offering resistance.' And every prisoner before whom he squirmed on his back would aim a blow at him with his boot, as though considering it his bounden duty. 'Look at that miserable cur!' the convicts used to say. But Belka dared not even howl, and if he felt the pain too much to be silent, would only utter a pitiful stifled yelp. In just the same way he would squirm before Sharik or any other dog whenever he ran out of the prison on his own affairs. He used to turn over on his back and lie there submissively whenever a big lop-eared mongrel rushed at him, barking wildly. But dogs like other dogs to be humble and submissive. The savage cur would be appeased at once, and would stand in a thoughtful kind of way over the humble animal lying there with his legs in the air and slowly and with immense curiosity begin to sniff him all over. What did the wriggling Belka think of during this time? 'Well what now? Is this ruffian going to tear me to pieces?' This was probably what came into his mind. But, after sniffing him carefully all over, the other dog finding nothing particularly remarkable, would give it up. Belka would jump up at once and again, limping, attach himself to the end of a long string of dogs escorting some pampered bitch."

Try not to wave the white flag too soon for your dog—let her choose her own surrender.

AGGRESSION An Akita about to attack curls her tail tighter while wagging it quickly very slightly from side to side. (See the illustration on p.61 for the Akita's tail at rest.)

the gentle arts of negotiation and diplomacy, find it difficult to interact normally with their canine pals and become increasingly nervy. One greyhound caretaker shrieks constantly when a canine pal chases her svelte, fit dog and they run making huge circles in the park. Her dog, hearing her shrieks, panics. The chaser, reverting to instinct, thinks that this must mean frightened prey. Chaos ensues. The caretaker desperately grabs her dog who becomes just a little more jittery every time. Another caretaker, when dogs bound up to him with a bark (a not-uncommon, "testing-the-water" canine approach) throws his body between his pampered pet and the approaching canine, convinced that his dog is about be savaged. How can this canine ever learn the real rituals of dogdom?

There are, of course, many reasons for canine aggression. One is that the dog is a professional doing her job to guard property or human. A guard dog with a kink at the end of her tail is intending to intimidate: She is waiting to see how you, or your dog react(s). A professional usually means business and, if you have strayed on to someone else's territory, to continue your advance will be interpreted by the dog as a challenge. It's definitely time to make a measured retreat using your knowledge of dog talk to the full. If the guard's ears strain forward or back against her head, she is staring at you, daring you "to make her day." If her mouth is opening ever-wider, and her snarling is becoming louder, an attack could be imminent. If her whole tail takes on a subtle S-like curve most likely the attack is definitely on its way. However, even now, a suitably submissive display indicating your lowly inoffensive status and strong desire to avoid conflict will normally avert danger (see box, right). Really, talking dog can be invaluable.

The other class of dog most likely to attack is composed of those that have been selectively bred by man to fight, such as pit bulls. These dogs, and others like them, are silent in attack and do not display the normal canine rituals. Journalist Stephen Budiansky, in his book *The Truth About Dogs*, writes: "the best advice I ever received for how to act if a predatory aggressive dog like a pit bull goes after you is just to ram your whole arm down his throat and hope he chokes to death: better that he gets your arm than your throat."

How to Avert Attack

Alan Beck, who carried out a fascinating study of feral dogs in Baltimore, recommends standing your ground and pretending to throw a hefty missile at the canine/canines in question—a maneuver that apparently stood him in good stead, but this might not prove so effective with large professionals, so try the following technique for more tried-and-tested results.

1. Most crucial is that under no circumstances should you turn and run, or scream. In every predator, from tiger to cat, from wolf to dog, running or screaming triggers a pursuit response followed by an attempt to bring the fleeing creature down—absolutely the last thing you want. In addition, avoid looking directly at an angry dog, which will provoke the canine equivalent of "What you staring at?"

2. Using your iron will to master the natural urge to flee, make yourself inoffensive. Look down and away and blink slowly. This is classic dog talk for "I really don't want to cause a problem." 3. Sometimes your submission will be the only sign the dog needs to defuse her anger, and she may walk away. However, if she holds her ground (as a professional guard dog may well do), just take a few really slow steps backward. If the dog doesn't move toward you, continue slowly moving backward and gradually turn your body sidewise. If the dog starts to follow you, turn slowly to face her, eyes averted, and blink slowly to reinforce the message that you really don't want trouble. Then, take a few more steps backward, gradually turn your body sidewise again and, oh-so-slowly, walk away, continually averting your gaze. Danger over.

FRIGHTENED, AGGRESSIVE DOG

Blinking slowly with averted gaze
can mollify an aggressive dog.

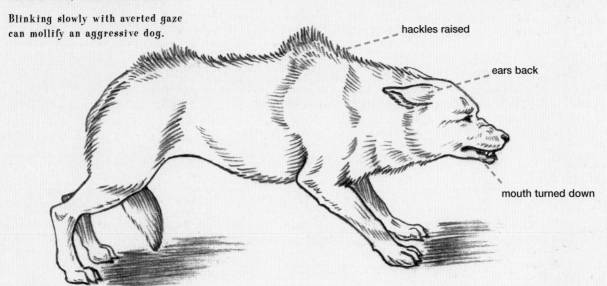

hackles raised

ears back

mouth turned down

Submission and Shyness

The opposite side to aggression and dominance in a dog is, of course, submission. However, the classic submission posture (see illustration, p.58) is not necessarily an expression of fear—it can be simply an acceptance of status and the status quo.

Implicit in this message is the fact that the groveler is not actually going to be hurt or attacked (at least if the superior being is dog, not human), because from this position it is impossible to flee or attack back. Wolves accept their position in the pack hierarchy, dogs their position in the park. You would not expect your own dog to adopt this posture with you unless she were apologizing for a major indiscretion and seeking to atone. As her superior in status, it behoves you to accept her grovel and take matters no further.

Dogs often employ the submissive position shown in the illustration below when dealing with humans they hardly know, but have no choice but to interact with—such as a caretaker's new friends. Recognizing that they must tolerate these humans and that the humans mean no actual harm, dogs will put up with being stroked on their stomachs and chests, but their feelings on the matter no doubt resemble those of a seven-year-old boy being smothered in kisses by an aging aunt. This is a stiff posture, the body is tense, and the tail is clamped over the genitalia. If the posture softens, the tail unfurls, the head relaxes, and the mouth becomes smiley. In other words the posture would begin to resemble that shown on page 58. Once the dog has adopted this more relaxed posture and is beginning to feel more at ease with you, a tentative friendship can now develop.

SUBMISSION A dog will adopt the submissive position with strangers they need to tolerate.

How to Gain the Trust of a Shy Dog

There are many sad, nervous dogs in animal shelters: Maybe you have decided to give one a home. How do you first gain her trust?

1. The first thing the dog needs to know is that you are not a threat. This means your movements need to be slow and easy. Direct stares and approaches will be interpreted as a challenge, increasing her nervousness and propensity to give empty snaps or run away. So, gently turn until you are sidewise to the dog and look unconcernedly away into the distance.
2. Having made yourself as inoffensive as possible, you may move into her general area, but not directly to her.
3. When you are a few feet (a meter or so) away from the dog, drop down to her level, still looking away. Hold out a tempting treat on the palm of your hand (dried liver is almost irresistible) and wait patiently for her to approach you. All the while whisper sweet nothings.
4. Soon you will feel a gentle, wet nose on your hand, the treat will be gone, and the process of friendship initiated. One or two treats later, she will probably feel secure enough to let you stroke her. Trust has been born.

averted gaze, slow blinking

delicious treat

SHY, NERVOUS DOG
Nervous animals are sensitive to sudden movement.

ears back

body lowslung

tongue licking at the air

Fear and Anxiety

Akitas will drop their tails when experiencing insecurity or apprehension; and wolf-type dogs will tuck their tails underneath their body (see illustrations, below).

A dog with a slightly lowered back, and bent legs is signaling insecurity or apprehension—they are either fearful or very, very nervous. Sometimes whippets will give this signal when they are close to a large dog, even one that is showing no signs of aggression or dominance and may not even have noticed them. Despite being a placatory and groveling posture, it does not, unlike the submissive postures, implicitly carry with it the expectation of not being harmed. This dog can still flee and bite if she must. Abused dogs often adopt this posture—fearful and appeasing, but expecting the worst. When out and about, the sudden adoption of this position means there is something potentially frightening on the horizon. Perhaps she has just seen a tribe of dog-walkers approach with their diverse groups, something not all canines

FEAR (1) Akitas will drop their tails when experiencing fear.

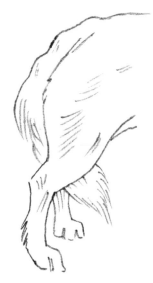

FEAR (2) When scared, wolf-type dogs will tuck their tails beneath the body.

relish; or has heard a strange crash in the undergrowth and is wondering whether or not to turn tail and run. The fearful position will be combined with pulled-back ears that move to garner further information about the situation, and the nostrils may open wider to take in subtle but important scent information. However, everything can change in a moment: If that strange noise in the woods turns out to be merely a friendly dog crashing through the undergrowth, her tail and ears will go up and her social life begins. However, if it turns out to be something unspecifically spooky, anxiety may turn into fear and then flight. Prior to fleeing, her ears will pull further back, her mouth will open slightly to reveal her teeth, her eyes will narrow, and her body poise for running. By quickly grabbing her collar the moment you see her ears go right back, you can avert disaster and prevent your dog from bolting, perhaps into the road. Fireworks are often the cause of this posture in dogs—if she has already heard one loud and frightening bang, the second will almost certainly cause her to run.

In a domestic situation where your dog is normally relaxed and happy, a straight back and lowish-slung tail swinging slowly (see illustration, right) can mean that she is depressed, sad, or even in pain. It's worth giving her a few moments of your time to consider what might be wrong. An Akita's way of signaling momentary pain is to drop her tail for a few seconds. If this happens while you are out walking and with a certain amount of regularity, the reason maybe the onset of the wear, and thus pain, associated with hip dysplasia, a not uncommon complaint in dogs of this breed.

PAIN/SADNESS A dog with a straight back and a lowish-slung tail that swings slowly from side to side could be feeling pain or sadness, or may be depressed.

ANXIETY A dog showing anxiety will pull her ears back, but keep them upright enough to be able to scout about for tell-tale sounds.

CHAPTER FOUR:

THE POWER OF TOUCH

"There is no psychiatrist in the world like a puppy licking your face."

Ben Williams (20th century)

Touch is powerful and intimate. It can heal and calm, create trust, or actively repulse, and yet demonstrate the most profound love. The brush of another's fingers on our wrist can cause electric shivers to run down our spine; while massage itself has the power to to release deep tension. Touching our pets, even through everyday petting and stroking, has untold benefits not only for our devoted animals, but also for us, their caretakers. In this chapter we learn to make the most of "talking" through touch.

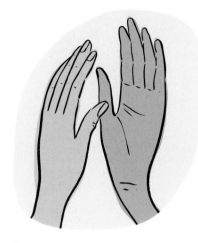

Shakespeare wrote of the "palmers' kiss"-the hand to hand touch that was the first expression of love between Romeo and Juliet.

As humans we are constrained from touching one another: Even the most intimate of companions can feel too nervous or embarrassed to ask for a hug or a cuddle, but to touch and be touched is to be human, and we suffer from skin hunger when we have not, for a while, felt the contact of another body with ours.

There is none of this constraint with dogs. Complete strangers roll on their backs demanding that we tickle their chests and rub their tummies—and usually we are more than happy to oblige. Dogs welcome our caresses, our pats, our scratches, and our strokes—who ever feared rebuff from the family labrador? And most dogs (certainly those who have not been forced by training to behave differently) feel free to show their affection to us in the same way.

In a competition held in the US, judges studied 1,105 photographs of families and their pets. In 97 percent of the photographs, the pet and human were touching and, usually had their heads very close together—a true sign of intimacy. Such is the physical intimacy of our relationships with our pets, that we can even recognize their bedding just from the way it smells. One researcher asked 26 dog-owners to smell two blankets, one impregnated with the odor of their own dog, the other with that of an unknown dog. Eighty-eight percent of the owners recognized their own canine's individual perfume. How many of us would be able to recognize the smell of even our closest human friends?

Stroking Dogs, Helping Humans

It is now well known that stroking dogs, and other animals, reduces blood pressure and that cohabiting with a pet radically increases the life span of coronary patients. In one study four times as many petless patients died in the year after leaving hospital than those with pets. But what people are less aware of is the reason for this. Dr. James Lynch, who has conducted ground-breaking research into the health benefits of animal companions, terms the reason for this dramatic statistic the "Physiology of Inclusion."

The Power of Love

When Detroit pet-owner Ruth Curry took her cat along to visit her father in a nursing home, she was simply amazed at the positive effect just being able to touch or hold the cat had, not only on her father, but on all the other residents, too.

Inspired by the visit, in 1985 she founded the charity "Pet-a-Pet," which provides pet-assisted therapy to those in need. Volunteer Tom Mondolis explains how working with his dog Dylan "opened up a whole new world of experiences for me ... . There was the woman who had suffered a stroke whose determination to grip Dylan's brush amazed me. There was the touching moment when a daughter rubbed her dying mother's hand with Dylan's paw ... ."

The Old Village School in Detroit is home to children with severe physical and mental impairments whose only opportunity to connect to the wider world is through Pet-a-Pet. Their supervisor said, "I don't believe I truly appreciated the impact the program had ... until I spent an hour with a child during a visit. Watching faces light up as the animals enter the room—the children roll and creep to get closer ... and small hands grasp at the animals' furry faces and ears—I realized how these animals bring joy and motivate the children to challenge their limitations."

What Lynch has discovered is that many people, even if they are not conscious of it, do not feel they belong in society or the greater living world around them so tend to react to everyday situations, such as talking to a neighbor, or hearing the squeal of a cat, as if they were a threat. Consequently, their bodies gear up for "flight or fight", increasing our blood pressure and heart rate, and diverting blood to the heart and muscles—a response which was only meant to be triggered by physical danger. In short, many people's blood pressure rises whenever they talk to a fellow human, and the more difficult they find communication in general, the steeper the rise. In time this leads to physiological exhaustion and a need to withdraw from others, which ironically only results in loneliness, premature disease and, ultimately, death. Lynch has termed this condition the "Physiology of Exclusion."

Lynch also found that blood pressure rises when we read aloud. However, in a study of children asked to read in front of a class, he discovered that, although the children's blood pressure rose at first, the simple presence of a pet dog brought it down again. Further, it was found that gazing at fish swimming in a tank caused blood pressure to drop more than conventional meditation.

Stroking our pets helps us to feel at one with the natural world, thus lowering our blood pressure.

Fascinated by the profound effect the natural world has on us, Lynch decided to experiment further with his daughter Kathleen and her beloved pet rescue dog, a schnauzer terrier called Rags. The astonishing results were broadcast in the US as a *Sixty Minutes* documentary. Kathleen sat quietly for three minutes and her blood pressure remained at its base level. She read poetry for two minutes and it increased greatly; then she was quiet again for another three minutes and her blood pressure returned to base. Rags was then put on her lap and she began to stroke him. As she did so her blood pressure fell by almost fifty percent from its peak to an entirely new and lower baseline level. In essence we can say that stroking Rags created a Physiology of Inclusion —a "biological state of enhanced relaxation, which draws people out of themselves and closer to others and the natural living world and which has a profound effect on people's hearts and blood vessels."

Stroking Dogs, Helping Dogs

Dogs crave touch too—perhaps for the same physiological, biological, and psychological reasons that we do. Lynch, who worked with lab dogs at the Johns Hopkins University School of Medicine in Baltimore, found that as soon as dogs were stroked or petted, their blood pressure fell dramatically.

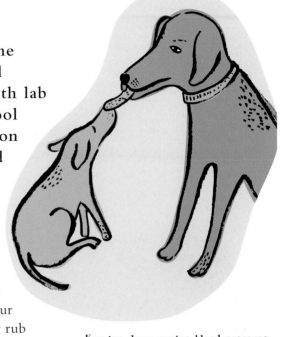

Keeping down canine blood pressure the easy way.

Puppies are constantly touched and licked by their mothers. At night they sleep securely, curled up with their warm siblings; by day they gambol constantly. When they come to live with us they simply want this tactile bliss to continue. When we return home they wag their entire bodies in greeting, lick our hands, our feet, our mouths—whatever is bare and available—and seductively rub their bodies along our legs hoping for reciprocal affection. If Lynch's work teaches us anything it is surely that to deny our dogs the tactile attention they crave is not only deleterious to our health, but to their health too.

To affirm our ties of affection and inclusion, my dog Poppy, having checked out that I really am where she thought I was, rubs my nose with hers, or, if that is out of reach, my hand or leg. She wakes me with a cold wet nose; if we go out for an unscheduled walk, she bounds with joy on the pavement then rubs her muzzle on my leg in canine thanks, just as she does when I present her with a new bone or toothsome treat. To elicit a tummy rub, she whines softly then lies on her back, legs furiously pumping through the air. The moment I stroke her belly, her legs flop, a look of beatific canine ecstasy adorns her face, and she becomes still. Wolf pups do this when having their bellies lick-massaged by their mothers to make them urinate and defecate—so, perhaps for canids a tummy rub stirs memories of maternal comfort, affection, and security.

Calming Sounds for Your Dog

Playing music (see pp.90–92) will help to calm nervous or hyperactive dogs. However, during research to see how 130 professional handlers soothed their dogs, Dr. Patricia McConnell (animal behaviorist and founder of Dog's Best Friend Ltd. in Wisconsin) also found that "long, continuous, flat, or descending noises" were the most successful. Adopting the dog's breathing rhythm is also useful, as it will both help you to assess your dog's mood and help her to relax.

Massaging Your Dog

Like us, dogs enjoy being massaged. However, while we might be happy for a massage to take an hour or so, dogs prefer a shorter routine: Fifteen or twenty minutes are usually more than adequate.

A truly mutually beneficial activity, massage will tone your dog's muscles, alleviate any stiffness she feels, improve her circulation, and eliminate toxins from her body; it will also greatly strengthen your existing bond. And, because massage creates feelings of security, and tranquility, it can, in time, create a connection with even the most nervous dogs.

There are some areas of her body that your dog will particularly love for you to stroke and massage because they are rich in nerve endings and particularly sensitive to touch. These are: her forehead and brow, her chest, the base of her lower back, and the bottom part of her tail. Some canines revel in a light touch,

PETRISSAGE This gentle kneading and stroking is a basic massage technique (see p.80).

which almost glides over their fur; some enjoy a firmer stroke, which hugs their body; others prefer a deeper pressure, which reaches the bones beneath their flesh. Experience will soon tell you what your dog enjoys. Before you begin massaging your dog, be sure to check for contraindications (see box, p.80), and do the pre-massage routine on pages 78–9.

The Massage Strokes: Effleurage

The fundamental movement of all massage is effleurage, a series of long, flowing, gentle strokes. Slow and light effleurage is soothing; but fast and light effleurage can be irritating. Deeper but slow effleurage helps drain the body's lymph and blood systems of toxins; while deep but faster effleurage strokes stimulate the muscles and are ideal to use before exercise. Gentle effleurage helps old, relatively inactive dogs keep their muscles flexible and imbues them with a sense of well-being, especially when combined with aromatherapy (see box, p.81).

Technique: Your hands should be relaxed and firm. Beginning just behind the ears, move your hands down the entire length of your dog's body and sides, toward her tail (both hands working in the same direction; see illustration, right), one side of the spine first and then the other (or, as a variation, you can place one hand on either side of the spine). Use your whole hand for this movement, not just your fingers, and make sure that the pressure is even on both sides of her spine.

EFFLEURAGE The masseuse's hands mold themselves correctly to the dog's body in effleurage (see left).

First Steps: Preparing for Massage

It is vital to take massage slowly, particularly at first. If your canine client shows any signs of restlessness, stop immediately—forcing her to have a massage is counterproductive and will end up frustrating you and her. If when massaging your dog you discover a hot spot, be careful—the muscle there may be inflamed or strained. Work carefully and if your dog seems in any distress consult your vet. Before using the techniques of effleurage (see p.77) and petrissage (pp.80–81), try the following general introduction to canine massage (it also makes a great pre-massage). At the start of any session approach your dog gently, offer her your open hand, and wait for her to nuzzle it in traditional canine greeting.

First Steps

Begin with passive touch—a technique in which the hand, palm down, is put on the muscle for between 30 and 90 seconds, warming the body and calming the soul. This is so non-invasive and non-threatening that even nervous dogs should remember the experience as comforting, and little by little become relaxed and healed under your touch. This technique also soothes acute wounds,

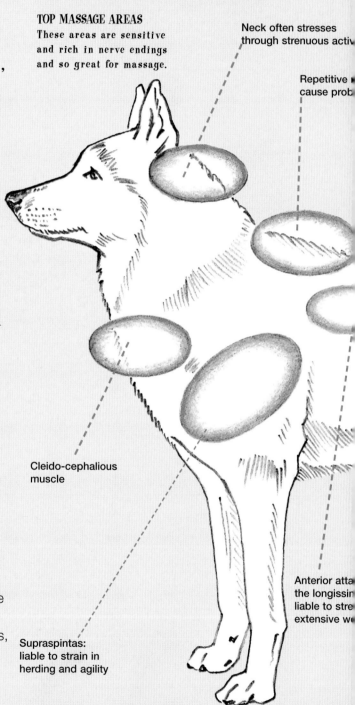

TOP MASSAGE AREAS
These areas are sensitive and rich in nerve endings and so great for massage.

Neck often stresses through strenuous activ

Repetitive cause prob

Cleido-cephalious muscle

Anterior atta the longissin liable to str extensive w

Supraspintas: liable to strain in herding and agility

Tension where the longissimus dorsi and the middle gluteal muscles join

Hip flexor muscles can strain easily

bruises, inflammation, and neuralgia (conditions where actually massaging the muscles is counterproductive). Tense, aggravated areas of the body hold excess heat. When our bodies are stressed or our muscles are tight a good massage temporarily drops our body temperature by one or two degrees, we may even shiver and feel chilly. As you rest the palm of your hand on the dog's afflicted area, warmth will radiate out as her flesh calms, bringing her tremendous relief.

A Simple Routine

1. Gently massage behind your dog's ears, with the tips of your fingers making circular movements—it is a rare dog that does not appreciate this luxurious and sensuous feeling.

2. If your dog seems happy, gently pull her ears through your fingers, lightly rubbing them as you do so. Some dogs have very sensitive ears and this technique may irritate them. If this is the case, stop immediately and move on to step 4.

3. Moving your hands gently, begin to massage your dog's neck at the base of the skull. Gradually move your hands down your dog's neck to her shoulder, gently squeezing and releasing the muscles as you do so. By now your dog should be very relaxed, her head down and forward in appreciation.

4. You could finish by rubbing gently behind the dog's ears with your index fingers for several seconds. Then, place your two index fingers where cold nose becomes warm flesh and slowly move your fingers up, past her eyes and then in two curves behind her eyebrows finishing at her temples where you make several clockwise circles. Repeat as often as your dog wants.

When Not to Practice Massage

Although massage is wonderfully helpful in so many situations, there are some in which it is very definitely contraindicated. These include but are not limited to when your dog:
• has a temperature—massage will accelerate blood circulation potentially increasing the temperature further;
• has any form of skin fungus, such as ringworm—massage can spread the affliction over her entire body;
• is in the acute stage of any infectious disease;
• has neuralgia, acute sprains, torn muscles, bruises, or any inflammatory conditions;
• is in shock.

And always check with your vet first if your dog has cancer, any type of tumor, or other medical condition, and never massage an area that is wounded.

The Massage Strokes: Petrissage

Another essential massage technique, petrissage comprises squeezing, kneading, and friction against the muscle (see illustration, below). Pressure and relaxation alternate in a smooth rhythm. When the movement is slow, it is soothing; when faster, it is stimulating. Kneading and squeezing muscle, much as you would dough, presses tissue into the body; while rolling skin and pulling the muscle moves tissue gently away from the body.

Petrissage is great for amateur and professional canine athletes alike, and helpful in the major muscular stress areas of the head and neck, hindquarters and legs, shoulders and forearms, and the back (see illustration, previous page)—all of which can be prone to knots and stiffness. As a dog uses his or her head and neck to balance, these areas are under constant strain whether the dog is running, catching balls and sticks in the park, competing in agility shows, or playing team Frisbee. As a result, massage to these areas is always beneficial.

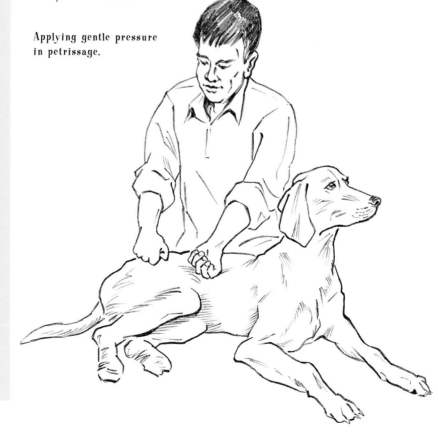

Applying gentle pressure in petrissage.

Techniques: The main stroke in petrissage is the kneading stroke. Practice this in much the same way you would knead dough, using the thumb and flat tips of your index, middle, and ring fingers. Make your movements gliding and rhythmical and use both hands at the same time. Use this stroke if you want to get into and release a muscle knot, and intersperse the kneading with soothing effleurage every thirty seconds or so.

To squeeze tense muscle in petrissage, put your whole hand on a congested area and then move the heel of your hand toward its fingers, gently squeezing the muscle upward. This can be very soothing on tense necks and backs if you squeeze once every second or so. Practiced fast, squeezing is good for warming up leg muscles when it is cold outside.

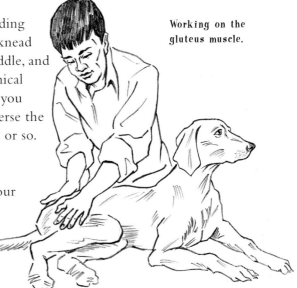

Working on the gluteus muscle.

Aromatherapy Massage for Older Dogs

Many older dogs suffer from arthritis. Massage combined with aromatherapy can really help them, alleviating pain and ridding their systems of the toxins that aggravate the condition. Valerie Worwood in her book *The Fragrant Pharmacy* suggests the following aromatherapy massage for canine arthritis:

1. Combine 4 drops of rosemary, 2 drops of lavender, and 3 drops of ginger oil in 1 fl. oz. (30ml) of a light vegetable oil, such as almond or jojoba.
2. Work the oil through the dog's coat and into the skin with a rhythmic movement starting from the haunches and moving inward. Work down the legs and along the spine, massaging the oil into all the vertebrae. After the massage your dog will lick off any excess oil, thus ensuring that the oils also reach her digestive system.
3. Worwood further advises half a teaspoon of White Clay (sometimes called kaolin) in your dog's water to help absorb any aggravating toxins lying in her intestine.

If your dog has rheumatism, try the same massage but this time use 5 drops of ginger, 2 drops of rosemary, and 5 drops of chamomile oil in 1 fl. oz. (30ml) of vegetable oil.

The Tellington Touch

Tellington TTouch (abbreviated to TTouch®), developed by championship horsewoman Linda Tellington-Jones, is different from massage. Instead of working on the body's muscular system, it concentrates on gently moving the skin with circular movements and lifts which activate the healing potential of the body by working at the cellular level, thus releasing fear and enhancing function.

When living creatures—be they canine or human—are tense, frightened, or in pain, their body develops specific habitual ways of responding. Neuroscientists such as American Dr. Candace Pert are beginning to uncover evidence that physical and emotional traumas are trapped in our body cells and conveyed to our brains by neurotransmitters. Tellington-Jones first worked with the creatures that surrounded her—horses— many of whom were labelled "aggressive" or "resistant." The profound discovery she made was that when she relieved the underlying cause of the horses' antisocial behaviour, usually pain or discomfort, by touching and moving their skin in

Before massage...

certain ways, their personalities were transformed. Since its formal beginnings in the 1970's, TTouch has been used to treat creatures as diverse as big cats, non-human primates, and humans (undergoing a TTouch session yourself can give you a real insight into how it will affect and help your dog).

How to Practice TTouch

The fundamental movement of TTouch is gentle and flowing. The practitioner places their hand lightly on the dog, gently bending the fingers so that the pads rest on the dog's skin. Circles are usually made in a clockwise direction with a light touch and relaxed wrist pushing the skin in one-and-a-quarter rotations, beginning at six and finishing at nine on an imaginary clock face. For general use the lines of circles should follow the lines of the body, and the fingers should slide along the skin, connecting each circle and keeping contact all the time.

For dogs who are exceptionally nervous, frightened, or in great pain, making the circular TTouches with the back of the hand will often gain their trust more readily. Dogs will usually have one or more body areas that they are reluctant for you to touch. With the circular TTouches you can release fear or pain

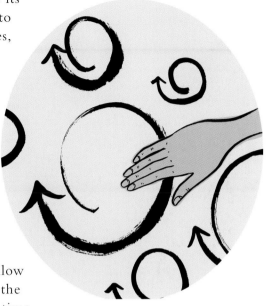

Tellington Touch consists of circles of movement, made with the fingertips. Each movement is one and a quarter circles, in a clockwise direction. The movement begins at "six o'clock" (as if on a clock face) and finishes at "nine o'clock."

...and after!

TTouch for Docked Dogs

Because dogs whose tails have been docked are incapable of moving the remaining stump normally, the attached muscle in their rectal area can weaken, which means they can suffer from incontinence. Many also suffer from phantom pain, as do human amputees, and still others hold their tails rigid because they retain locked-in memory of fear and pain. And, because dogs are stoical about pain, probably as a survival mechanism, humans and vets do not realize how much pain these dogs suffer. TTouch can help these conditions. Moving the tail stump in tiny circles—a non-habitual movement—will relax both the stump and muscle, which widens the dog's range of motion and adds confidence. And, applied to the stump, Raccoon TTouches, which push the skin in a circle and a quarter using the lightest touch with the tips of the fingers, remove pathological pain.

in such areas and change behavior. As trust builds between you and the dog, she will gradually let you touch those areas, allowing you to release the hurt.

Tense, assertive, or angry dogs tend to hold their heads stiff and upright. TTouches and sliding strokes on their ears help a dog to relax the neck and change the posture, which in turn releases fear and breaks this physical pattern. The dogs will lower their heads and relax their necks, a body posture that automatically causes them to relax.

When to Use TTouch

Vets and behaviorists are increasingly disposed to use drugs to treat even quite minor psychological and behavioural problems in dogs, such as a fear of thunder and lightning, as well as graver problems such as those caused by earlier abuse. (See Chapter Two for further discussion on so-called behavioral problems in domestic dogs.) Medication prevents these dogs from exhibiting fear but the thunder and lightning, or the memory of their abuser still frightens them. TTouch, because it releases locked-in fear and tension, alters the way dogs feel about great thunderclaps and violet zig zags renting the sky, or past abusive experiences. In short, the dogs are no longer frightened or anxious. TTouch can also break a host of common problem patterns from canine car-sickness to barking.

Chronic and pathological pain also responds well to TTouch. Jake, a beautiful, alert, intelligent German shepherd, had four crumbling vertebrae—just too many to make operating a viable option. He also suffered from severe arthritis, as well as numbness in his hindquarters and tail. Besides being vital for balance and gait, the muscles which move the tail have their origins deep in the dog's rectal area and are continuous with both the pelvic and rectal muscles, and if they aren't used correctly, urinary and fecal incontinence can develop, as can weakness in the pelvic diaphragm. Jake clearly needed all the help he could get so besides putting him under conventional veterinary care his human asked TTouch practitioner Marie Miller to work with him. TTouch on Jake's tail reminded his nervous system that his tail was still there. This, combined with other TTouch work, both kept his digestion steady and staved off incontinence until a very short time before he died. It also relieved his chronic pain and gave him a much greater feeling of emotional well-being.

Working with TTouch can genuinely transform, by awakening your dog's own healing energies and powers of regeneration. It is important to work non-judgmentally—in other words to place no pressure on you or your dog. Instead, celebrate every tiny positive change, and remember, as Tellington-Jones herself says, TTouch is "as practical, accessible, and real as your own two hands. All it takes is your desire, your love, some trust in your intuition and, of course, a little practice."

The TTouch Body Wrap: Sensing the Body

Another arm of TTouch is the body wrap—a light, wide elastic bandage, which is crossed over the dog's body closely, but not tightly. The physical sensation of the wrap gives canines a sense of their own body—just as we might suddenly become very conscious of our arms if we were to don a close-fitting jumper after months of wearing sleeveless tops. This allows dogs suffering from balance and mobility problems, such as Jake (see opposite), to improve the way they move, and changes the habitual posture of fearful dogs, who hold the base of their tails, their legs, and their shoulders very tightly, thus releasing their negative emotions.

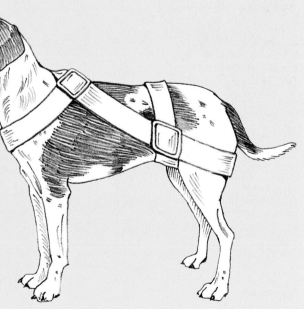

CHAPTER FIVE:

YOUR DOG'S SUBTLE SENSES

"I've seen that look in dogs' eyes, a quickly vanishing look of amazed contempt and I am convinced that basically dogs think humans are nuts." John Steinbeck (1902–68)

In this chapter we look at how our own moods and behavior affect those of our dogs, as well as the fascinating possibilities of canine telepathy, and dogs communicating from beyond the grave. Mood and character are created by complex mixtures of emotion, physiology, genetics, psychology, and external forces; and mood can be infectious. This increased perception can affect pets as well as people. Dogs pick up on moods-it would be extraordinary if the towering presence of canine caretakers had no effect on their charges' psychology and behavior. If anxiety is present in a family, their pets may develop gastric upsets or even seizures.

Two-hundred-and-eighty-five English cocker-spaniel caretakers were asked to complete a personality questionnaire. This study revealed that those whose dogs had already been classed as highly aggressive were "significantly more likely to be tense, less emotionally stable, shy, and undisciplined" than those whose cockers had been classed as low in aggression. There may, of course, be several explanations for this. Looking after an aggressive dog is a task fraught with difficulty, inclined to stress out even the most steady humans; less emotionally stable people may be more sensitive to subtle signals of aggression; or perhaps living with a tense, shy human makes the dog feel both nervous and protective. Guide dogs solving their human's problems (see pp.41–2) exhibit the same protective urge in a different form.

Research at the Royal School of Veterinary Studies, Edinburgh, found that many dogs with serious behavioral "problems," including biting, were simply responding to conflict states and over-arousal induced by their caretakers. This type of research is scarce, which makes the case history given on the following page (recorded by Valerie O'Farrell, one of the Edinburgh researchers) particularly important.

Dogs and their Phobias

Suffering from agoraphobia (fear of open spaces), Miss A asked O'Farrell to visit her at home. Her problem? Pearl, her nine-month-old corgi, was frightened of leaving the house and, having urinated or defecated, would not even linger in the garden.

Walks around the street were taken with reluctance, and if let off her leash in a park, Pearl dashed for home. Miss A claimed that Pearl's agoraphobia was due partially to her having fallen onto her head off a low wall aged four months, and partially to having been accidentally shut alone in a room while a window cleaner went about his work. Miss A apparently found the dog trembling behind a sofa and claimed that, after this experience, Pearl was particularly afraid of metallic noises that sounded like the clanking of the window cleaner's ladder. Although this curious synchronicity could have occurred by chance, it is quite hard to imagine that it did. Agoraphobia rarely afflicts canines. Those who most closely observed Miss A, her friends, were convinced that her own fearfulness had made Pearl afraid, too. Besides, being frightened when shut in seems more likely to give rise to claustrophobia than agoraphobia. But by blaming Pearl's problem on external events, Miss A managed to avoid taking any responsibility for her plight. O'Farrell posits that because she empathized with Pearl, Miss A "did not force the dog into phobic situations and so increased her fear." Far more likely, this was a perfect excuse for Miss A to stay at home, enabling her to blame the dog for her own phobic behavior. Ali Taylor, chief Behaviorist at Battersea Dogs' Home, says that, in her experience, phobias being passed from human to dog is very common; a fear of thunder and lightning being a good example. If humans are scared when clouds loudly collide, they quite naturally imagine their canine may also be frightened and rush to comfort them . But, says Taylor, this gives the dog the idea that something is really wrong; for why otherwise would they be offered solace? Far better to just behave as normal. The dog should then just accept thunder as just another noise in her world.

Communicating through Music

Music can elicit powerful emotions and a host of subconscious activity in the parts of our nervous system which, in evolutionary terms, are the most primitive—our heart and respiration, circulation, and skin conductivity. It also seems to activate the cortical systems associated with emotion. Listening to grunge rock music, for example, induces various moods ranging from hostility to tension; meditation music on the other hand can propel the listener to another plane.

Music is a powerful medium, which is able to conjure up all kinds of emotions in humans. Dogs have emotional responses to music, too.

At first glance emotion induced by music seems to have no particular benefit for our survival, so why did this reaction evolve? One explanation is that music helps provide social cohesiveness— a contemporary example being the singing and chanting of British soccer fans. Music can heighten arousal and induce bonding—many peoples have used music to inspire their warriors before battle. Conversely, it also lowers arousal by diminishing testosterone levels, which reduces group conflict and sexual competitiveness. A baby's survival capacity is dependent upon the strength of its bond with its mother—a mother singing or talking in a "sing-song" voice to her infant, before the baby can express him- or herself verbally, generates feelings of emotion for both mother and child, and intensifies the parental bond.

If language is part of the mind's general facility for learning and memorizing and, as such, not the exclusive province of humans (see pp.45–7), and if music is language's precursor, then it is reasonable to assume that animals also have the capacity to react emotionally to music. Perhaps then there is truth to the colloquialism that music soothes the savage beast.

Finding the Rhythm of Calm

Dogs in even the most benevolent of rescue centers are under great stress. Their lives are unpredictable and filled with noise, and humans frequently scrutinize and stare at them. If music could relax these dogs, it would benefit the dogs and their carers, and make them more desirable to potential rescuers.

Researchers, sponsored by The National Canine Defence League in the UK, played rescue dogs different sounds for four hours at a time on alternating days. The control sound was the everyday noise at the kennels; the second was radio chat shows which contained no music; the third a randomly chosen selection of classical music; the fourth was music by the heavy metal band Metallica; the fifth was light pop music from a chart-hits compilation.

Both the heavy metal and the classical selection had profound effects on the dogs. Metallica stirred their emotions to such a degree that they barked constantly (Ali Taylor, the chief behaviorist at London's Battersea Dogs' Home told me that both heavy metal and heavy rock made her group more generally hysterical); while classical music soothed the troubled beasts, relaxing them and inducing them to lie down and rest contentedly.

Classical music has been shown to calm nervous dogs. Try it at home!

Is Your Dog a Music-lover?

Those of you with restless dogs, camcorders, and *Petsound* (see p.92), Mozart, or any other soothing music, might like to test the theories for yourselves.

1. Set up the video recorder, switch off any music, and leave your dog firmly home alone for around an hour and half.
2. A few days later repeat the experiment but this time allow your home to vibrate gently to the strains of your chosen music.
3. Watch the tape back and compare and contrast your canine's behavior patterns.

CDs for Humans or Dogs?

Petsound is a CD produced by human behaviorists, in collaboration with Ali Taylor and the canines and workers at Battersea. The producers of *Petsound* are insistent, against an increasing body of evidence, that their album is designed to relax the human half of the canine–person partnership and by doing so transfer their sense of calm to the dog, as opposed to the music influencing the dog directly.

I fell fast asleep while listening to *Petsound* so it certainly soothed me. I then played it to two extremely excitable and diminutive terriers, Clara and Millie. A bouncing bundle of ginger-brown vivacity, Millie deals with large dogs, such as my dog Poppy, by barking excitedly at them and exhibiting low-level, nervous aggression. Interestingly as *Petsound* played Millie lay on her back in a relaxed manner, allowed Poppy to sniff her all over, and then pottered off about her canine business. Was this coincidence triggered by a change in the mood of the humans present at the time (Clara and Millie's human, and me)? Or was it a direct response by the dog to the music? We will never know for sure, but why not conduct your own experiments at home to see how your dog reacts? If you can't get hold of *Petsound*, use any music that you find relaxing and try to judge whether your dog relaxes just because you relax, or whether the music induces a canine state of calm directly.

Quin and The Unchained Melody

Quin, a restless English springer spaniel who, when at home, constantly runs in circles and dashes in and out of his garden, is one of the many canines entrusted to Margaret, a professional dog-walker. Margaret avoids commercial music to calm Quin and instead sings him The Righteous Brothers' *Unchained Melody*. After three or four lines, Quin, who initially sits up attentively, begins to yawn. Margaret looks at him, gives him a cuddle, and continues. Three lines later Quin yawns again. At the line "lonely rivers flow to the sea," he lies down and yawns. Thirty seconds later his head is down and he is fast asleep. Is this mood-transference? Hypnotism? Mesmerism? Or is it a direct result of the music? Whatever the reason it never fails.

Canine Telepathy and Otherworldliness

The existence of paranormal powers and telepathy are fiercely contested by the scientific community. Skeptics ask what evolutionary purpose does it serve? In an urban society, particularly one in which everyone owns a cellphone, its purpose is not obvious but, as Dr. James Serpell of the University of Pennsylvania writes in *Companion Animals and Us* (edited with A.L. Podberscek and E.S. Paul), "an ability to tune into and resonate with the lives of other organisms via internalized animals within may, indeed, be part of our biological heritage, an evolved mental skill that once enhanced our survival as hunters and gatherers."

True hunters, such as the Kalahari Bushmen, whose very lives depend upon the success of their hunt, have always empathized with the animal they need to kill, respecting the animal's sacrifice so that they might live. The Bushmen believe that no matter how skilled they are, unless the animal willingly sacrifices itself it can never be killed. And so, for a period before and during hunting, the Bushmen calculate their every thought and every emotion, and even the slightest of actions, to make a supremely intimate mental bond with their prey.

Contemporary technological society, which is based on speed of communication, in evolutionary terms has hardly begun, and as organisms we are still firmly based in the biological age. Even fifteen years ago there was no email, twenty years ago no cellphones, a hundred and twenty years ago no land lines, two hundred years ago no organized mail. In societies without these forms of communication, the evolutionary benefits of telepathy

The Power of Thought

Lieutenant Colonel J.H. Williams, working with elephants deep in the Burmese jungle in the early twentieth century, discovered a curious affinity with his German shepherd Molly Mia. Human and companion traversed the wild forests together and to amuse Molly Mia, Williams sometimes left objects back at camp, which he would send a joyful Molly Mia to retrieve. If Williams was engaged in dangerous work, such as blasting boulders, he would leave Molly Mia at base. However, no matter how much he concentrated on his task, a distinct picture of Molly Mia "sitting on her haunches, watching for me, listening either for the sound of my voice or some noise in the jungle, a sign that I had come back" constantly came into his mind. Then one evening Williams accidentally discovered that she would obey him, even when he wasn't looking at or speaking to her: "She was shaking the bamboo floor of the jungle hut and I thought, 'For goodness sake lie down,' and she lay down. It was something so unconscious that I couldn't quite be sure that I hadn't thought out loud. I tried my first experiment. I went on with my work, but I willed Molly Mia to come to my side, and she immediately got up and came to my side."

Williams began to will her to come to him from longer and longer distances, starting with a hundred yards (100m) from camp and gradually increasing the distance to two miles (3.25km). Every time, just as if she had heard him call, Molly Mia appeared directly.

He then devised a particularly arduous task. Having synchronized his watch with the camp clock, Williams set off into the forest, first crossing a river and, then crucially re-crossing it. Six hours later, at noon and four miles (6.5km) away, Williams "withdrew from my Burmans and sat down and concentrated hard on Molly. Within half an hour I heard her ranging somewhere near me, and towards me she came bounding in a minute or two. The most interesting thing about this was that my servant Aung Net told me that at noon Molly Mia had dashed off exactly as if she had heard me call: but she did not cross the river."

become obvious. Imagine a shepherd out alone, leg broken at the bottom of a ravine. If he were able to convey his plight by mental image to his dog or a member of his community he could be saved. Dr. Aristide Esser, a psychiatrist and neurologist at the Rockland State Hospital, New York, carried out some experiments that give credence to the theory that human and beast can communicate telepathically.

Proving Canine Telepathy

Two boxer dogs, a mother and son, were trained to cower at a raised, rolled newspaper. They were then placed in separate, copper-lined isolation chambers that were impervious to vibration, soundproof, and in different areas of the hospital. Through the observation panel researchers, watching as the son was threatened with the newspaper and cowered, also saw his mother, oblivious to her son's situation, cower at exactly the same moment.

Dr. Esser also placed the master of a hunt in one isolation chamber and two of his beagles in another. Slides of various animals were displayed on the chamber's wall and the master of the hunt "shot" them with an air rifle. As he did so the beagles "went wild barking and whining just as they would on a real hunt." Was it coincidence, or demonstration of a very useful sense?

Powers that were once taken for granted are now regarded as fantasy because on one level contemporary society no longer needs these powers; and on another level because people don't wish to be associated with what is generally considered to be primitive or "unscientific." But, when far away from telephones and the mail, these powers can surface naturally (see box, opposite).

One of the first scientists to investigate canine–human telepathy was Professor W. Bechterev, working in Russia during the 1940's. His subject was "a very lively and nimble" circus fox terrier named Pikki. Pikki's owner Vladimir Durow describes his telepathic technique, which I quote on the following page in full just in case you feel you have the necessary stamina to follow his recommendations!

"Suppose we have the following task: to suggest that the dog go to a table and fetch a book lying upon it. I call him and he comes. I take his head between my hands as if I am symbolically inculcating in him the thought that he is entirely in my power ... I fix my eyes upon his ... I pull together all my nerve power and concentrate so that I entirely forget the outer world, impressing upon myself mentally the outlines of the object in which I am interested [in this case the table and book] to such an extent that even when I look away it stands before me as though real. In the course of about half a minute I literally devour the object with my eyes, think of its minutest details ... . Enough! I have memorized them. I turn the dog toward myself with an imperious gesture and look into his eyes, somewhere into his interior. I fix into his brain what I just before fixed into my own. I mentally put before him the part of the floor leading to the table, then the legs of the table, then the tablecloth and finally the book. The dog begins to get nervous, to become restless, tries to get loose. Then I mentally give him the command or rather the mental push 'Go!' He tears himself away like and automaton, approaches the table, seizes the book with his teeth. The task is done."

Flushed with his triumphs with Pikki, which were many and well-documented, Bechterev began to command telepathically his own dog Gabish to leap on to a variety of chairs. Tragically Gabish's career was cut short when "after missing a leap," he "sprained his shoulder and began to limp badly."

Reading Your Mind

Many individuals insist that the animals are telepathic. Even that guru of practical training, the UK's Barbara Woodhouse wrote, "You should always bear in mind that the dog picks up your thoughts by an acute telepathic sense and it is useless to be saying one thing and thinking another, you cannot fool a dog … . A dog's mind is so quick at picking up thoughts that as you think them they enter the dog's mind simultaneously."

When training a dog it is essential to believe that she can do what you ask. This is doubly important if you are trying to establish a telepathic rapport with her. Many people fail with training simply because they are sending the dog mixed messages: "Attempt to do this task, even though I don't think you'll manage it." This undermines her confidence, her ability, and above all her willingness to try.

"Speaking" to the dog using only telepathic communication, Russian professor W. Bechterev successfully trained his research dog Pikki to retrieve a book from a table.

Joseph Wylder, a scientist and canine behaviorist, suggests that telepathic and behavioral training are combined. So, as you teach your puppy to sit by pushing on her backside and saying "sit," you also constantly think the command even when not speaking it.

From this, progress to talking to your dog—tell her what you are doing while you wash the dishes or bake a cake. She won't exactly understand what you mean, but she will know that the communication is meant for her and, as she has a predisposition to want to understand you, she will make every effort to gain sense from your words and perhaps in time begin to pick up your silent willed thoughts.

Just as importantly, you need to be able to translate your dog's reactions. This means understanding every nuance of her body language, from how her ears twitch when she sees a squirrel to how she cocks her head on one side when you speak to her. Note how she responds to absolutely everything you say to her out loud. Soon you will find that you can judge if, and how, she is reacting to your silent communications.

It is also vital to be open to your dog's mind. If you think that your dog has sent you a message, take a chance: Respond and see what

"One day while at work it started to thunder and rain. As I worked I became increasingly edgy. Then very agitated. Something was wrong. At this point I will add that I never took time off work. I asked my employer if I could take the afternoon off, I didn't feel quite right. On my way home I knew Eric, my German Shepherd, was in trouble, I knew he was bleeding. When I arrived home I rushed to the back patio. The window was broken. Frightened, Eric had hit the glass with his paw and sliced off the front pads on broken glass. He was bleeding very badly. I feel he needed me and called out the only way he could—telepathically—knowing I would come home to him."

Many owners report that, like Kane, their dog is waiting patiently for them at the window when they return home.

happens. You may open a new interspecies communication—one far more meaningful than speech. It may also save her life: The example above is from *Dogs Who Know When Their Owners are Coming Home* by Rupert Sheldrake.

Five-hundred-and-eighty people wrote to Rupert Sheldrake (see also box, opposite) describing how their dogs knew they were coming home. Having scrutinized these case studies, Dr. Sheldrake was forced to conclude that neither auditory nor olfactory cues triggered the dog's information and that some other sense must be responsible. He has conducted many trials to establish the veracity of this phenomenon, the most recent being with Kane, a Rhodesian ridgeback whose human traveled more than five miles (8km) away from home and then returned home randomly, or when asked to do so by pager. Meanwhile Kane remained at home, while being filmed continuously by time-coded videotapes. In nine out of ten trials, Kane spent 26 percent of his time at the window while his human was returning but only one percent of the rest of the time there.

And it isn't just Kane who knows when his owner is coming home. So do HM Queen Elizabeth II's personally trained gun dogs at her house at Sandringham in Norfolk. "All the dogs in the kennels start barking the moment she [the Queen] reaches the gate—and that is half a mile away. We don't know how they can tell and they don't do it with anyone else," said head gamekeeper Bill Meldrum in an interview with the magazine *Country Life*.

An argument constantly employed by canine-telepathy skeptics is that dog-caretakers' memories are not to be trusted; that they remember only the rare, "coincidental" occasions when their dog is waiting for them at the window, and forget the thousands of occasions on which this does not happen. You need to judge for yourselves whether or not your dog is telepathic. Try the exercise below and that on page 101 as a starting point.

Is Your Dog Telepathic?

Dr. Rupert Sheldrake, a biologist and author who has extensively researched the paranormal, suggests this easy experiment to discover whether or not your dog is telepathic.

1. Put your dog outside or in a separate room where she definitely can't hear or see you.
2. Set up a video camera to film yourself, ensuring that the time code will record onto the tape.
3. With the tape running, at random moments make a note of the time and call your dog telepathically. If she appears soon after the call in a number

of tests, but does so significantly less at other times, this is pretty good proof of real telepathic communication.

Sensing Presence

Of course, animals also communicate with one another. Wolf expert Barry Lopez observed the following: "I have noticed that captive animals at rest seem to pick up cues from each other even though there is no audible sound and they are out of visual contact. Their backs may be turned to each other or one may be off in some trees in a corner of the pen. When one animal stares intently at something, for example, it apparently creates some kind of tension. Other animals respond by lifting their heads and turning without hesitation to look at the area where the first animal is staring. In my experience it was most often the subordinate animals that responded first, and the alpha animals last. Perhaps further research will establish a firmer foundation for this. It hints of course, at much." Is this another form of telepathy? In the wild silent communication could alert pack members to danger, while their foe would have no idea—undoubtedly, an extremely useful survival mechanism.

A high percentage of adults and children believe in the sense of being stared at and this belief significantly increases with age, causing shocked skeptic Gerald Winer at Ohio State University to write it is "as if irrationality were increasing rather than declining between childhood and adulthood." But perhaps the truth is that people experience this phenomenon so often that they come to believe in it implicitly and accept it as a normal part of life. Science took a very long time to discover that bats navigate using echolocation, and that butterflies see ultraviolet, but these phenomena were always there, science just didn't realize it. Perhaps discovering what is behind the sense of being stared at just requires researchers to think more broadly. In an informal survey conducted in Europe and the US, Rupert Sheldrake asked people if they had ever found that they could stare at an animal from behind and make it turn round. Fifty-five percent answered yes. Of course, in evolutionary terms sensing when you were being stared at could mean the difference between life and death.

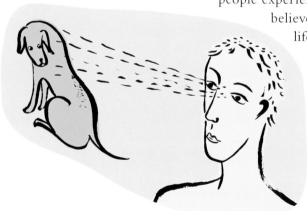

Many people find that their animals are able to sense when they are being stared at-be careful where you lay your gaze!

Dogs from Beyond the Grave

Dogs possess so many unusual powers—from demanding their dinner at the dot of six—a phenomenon so common that it is not even considered remarkable—to knowing when their humans have died. However, I close this chapter with the most contentious claim of all—that dogs are able to present themselves as ghostly apparitions—and leave you to determine its veracity.

A Mrs. Sebium, staying with friends in north London, followed an ancient tradition by walking in their garden repeating "fantastic words" while "sprinkling hempseed lavishly." Hearing a pattering on the gravel path behind her, she turned to see an "ugly," black-and-tan mongrel running enthusiastically toward her. However, when she put her hand down to prevent him jumping on her dress, "Mongrel" melted away into thin air.

Six months later, at home in Bath, southwest England, Mrs. Sebium saw the identical dog scampering across the lawn, happily wagging his tiny tail. However, this time Mongrel was flesh and blood. Mrs. Sebium's heart melted and the dog became her own. Three happy years later she visited friends, this time in southeast London, to celebrate Halloween, leaving Mongrel safely at home. At eleven at night she retired to her room and was amazed when, drawing back the hangings of her four-poster bed, she saw Mongrel on the counterpane. However, poignantly and unusually "His ears hung, his mouth dropped, and his bleared little eyes were watery and sad." She put out her hand to comfort him, but his diminutive form immediately vanished. Two days later she received a letter saying that Mongrel had been run over and killed, at eleven at night, on Halloween…

Does Your Dog Know When You are Coming Home?

If you have a camcorder, set it up when going out on a non-routine mission, such as visiting a friend, to see whether or not your dog knows when you are on your way home.

1. Set up the camera with a wide panorama of your window (or door, depending on where your dog might wait).
2. Synchronize your watch with the camcorder's timer, and leave.
3. While you are out note the time when: you decide you are coming home; you start coming home; and you actually return home.
4. Check your times with the tape to see if your dog anticipates your arrival (when you made the decision or began your return)—or whether she remains snoring next to the radiator until she hears your key in the door.

CHAPTER SIX:

THE SECRET LIFE OF DOGS

"Each individual has to do what he or she needs to do in her or his own world."

Marc Bekoff, *Minding Animals* (2002)

We ask so much of our pet dogs. If left alone they must display infinite patience, and even suffer criticism should loneliness turn to boredom and they chew the furniture. We expect them to indulge our children, who may playfully poke them or pull their tails. But the dog, left to her own devices, is far from passive. She has places to go, friends to visit, pals to play with, food caches to investigate, and enemies to despatch; in short, a complex daily agenda to rival ours. In this chapter we discover how this free spirit, with his or her own agenda, can survive very happily without any help from us at all.

As a technological society we seem to be adopting a certain fear of nature; our obsession with "safety" has never been greater. The result is that the poor dog, nature's domestic ambassador, gets a very raw deal.

As a dog-lover how often have you seen over-cautious parents gather their children into their arms at the mere sight of a dog? And our concerns over hygiene have led to the barring of our dogs from bars and cafés. Our material society means that dogs from more affluent homes may be inundated with physical luxuries, but it should not be at the expense of exercise. If you provide adequate physical and mental stimulation for your dog, many behavioral problems may not develop. In the event problems have occurred, exercise can help reduce them. The right kind of exercise is important, too: an hour's walk on a leash is not as beneficial to a dog as a mentally stimulating 20-minutes' worth of unrestrained ball play in a garden.

Take this real-life scenario. A woman with a beautiful and affectionate, sandy-colored mongrel, works at home, seeing clients from 7AM until 9PM—in other words 14 hours a day. She does this for six days a week. Her dog, let's call her Cassie, has a walk at around 6 or 7AM, and after that is left unattended in a comfortable house until a dog-walker comes at three for one hour, after which Cassie is left to her own devices again until nine. Cassie is thoroughly miserable, and understandably begins to see the clients as people who are taking her mistress away from her. So she starts to nip them—apparently without provocation. In order to prevent this happening, Cassie is confined to one room. However, the biting escalates to the street outside, where people whom Cassie thinks might be visiting her mistress are given clear warnings (through increasingly hearty bites) to stay away. In turmoil, Cassie's owner festoons the dog with behavior-pattern interrupters, shouts at her, and blames the dog-walker for the dog's antisocial behavior, but doesn't see (or accept) that Cassie's behavior is the result of boredom, frustration, and loneliness. All Cassie really needs is lots of love and attention and many happy hours rolling in mud, chasing squirrels, and socializing with her canine peers.

Before cars dominated the landscape, threatening paw and more, and people did not instinctively regard a lone dog as a threat or dog feces as a dangerous chemical, much-beloved canines ranged wild and free, returning to their home only for supper or a relaxing snooze by the fire. The tale below (originally written in 1877) illustrates perfectly those halcyon days.

"... in the course of my friend's walk he turned into a baker's shop and bought a bun. As he stood at the door of the shop eating his bun, a large dog came to him and begged for a share, which he got, and seemed to enjoy, coming back for piece after piece. 'Does the dog belong to you?' my friend asked of the shop woman. 'No,' she answered, 'but he spends most of his time here, and begs halfpennies from the people who pass.' 'Halfpennies! What good can they be to him?' 'Oh he knows very well what to do with them; he comes into the shop and buys cakes.' This seemed rather a remarkable instance of cleverness even for the cleverest of animals, so by way of testing its reality, my friend went out of the shop into the street, where he was immediately accosted by the dog, who begged for something with all the eloquence of which a dog is capable. He offered him a halfpenny, and was rather surprised to see him accept it readily, and walk, with the air of a regular customer, into the shop, where he put his forepaws on the counter, and held out the halfpenny towards the attendant. The young woman produced a bun, but that did not suit the dog, and he held his money fast 'Ah,' she said, 'I know what he wants,' and took down from a shelf a plate of shortbread. This was right; the dog paid his halfpenny, took his shortbread, and ate it with decorous satisfaction. When he had quite finished he left the shop, and my friend much amused, followed him, and when he again begged, found another halfpenny for him, and saw the whole process gone through again." *The Spectator Book of Dog Stories*

A Canine Love Story

Gustav, a large, strong, and determined bloodhound, was from time to time able to break free from the confines of his town garden and range wild and free on the local land. On one such occasion Gustav happened upon a beautiful bitch on heat, but human intervention terminated Gustav's courtship and his delectable darling was chauffeured away to her home some several miles away. Gustav, however, did not give up on finding love. Using his acutely honed tracking ability, he followed his darling's trail through traffic to her million-dollar home, where he dejectedly paced the pavements until, at last, a local resident called his owner to come to fetch him.

Back in those long-gone days behavioral problems in dogs were few and far between because, as British vet and author Bruce Fogle so succinctly puts it, "they were allowed to act like dogs"—and dogs have their own agendas.

We know very little of the dog's true desires or natural behavior because most pet dogs have little or no opportunity to act them out—although occasionally they still manage to escape from their owner's custody and take matters into their own paws (see box, left).

But throughout the world there are vast numbers of feral dogs (that is, dogs who have been born and bred on the streets), strays, and pets on day release—usually in poor neighborhoods—whose fascinating and intricate lives speak volumes for canine sagacity, tenacity, emotion, ingenuity, altruism, and intelligence, revealing more of their essential motive than any laboratory experiment. Many of us are concerned about these dogs—both for us and for the dogs themselves. We might worry about public health issues or the apparent cruelty shown toward dogs living on the streets, lacking as they do, veterinary care, warm soft beds, and an ample

Dogs in Bharatpur roll joyfully, happy to be free.

Feral dogs are resourceful—they
always know where to find food.

Science Doesn't Always Know Best

Sadly, many pound dogs are used for scientific experiment. In the quotation that follows (from Marc Bekoff's *Minding Animals*), scientists perform an experiment on a dog that, in fact, teaches us nothing we don't already know about human or animal behavior, begging the question: Why do it?

"When a normal, naïve dog receives escape/avoidance training in a shuttle box, the following behavior typically occurs: At the onset of electric shock the dog runs frantically about defecating, urinating, and howling until it scrambles over the barrier and so escapes from the shock .... However in dramatic contrast ... a dog who has received inescapable shock while strapped in a Pavlovian harness soon stops running and remains silent until the shock terminates. It seems to 'give up' and 'passively accept' the shock."

supply of scientifically-balanced dry food. But, really, who are we to judge? The happiest dogs I have ever seen are two feral dogs in Bharatpur, Rajasthan. Creamy white mongrels with startling green eyes, they lived on the fringes of a hotel where there was food a-plenty. Their favorite game was to frolic on a huge mountain of sand sacks, which were one day destined to become guest rooms. Up and down they ran for hours every day, playing "king of the castle," rolling down the sandy hill, and clambering up again before finally falling into a well-earned sleep or scavenging some leftover chicken tikka.

Usually chased from the hotel's grounds by the gardener, who feared for his exotic and luxuriant flowerbeds, the dogs were granted temporary immunity from his wrath when sitting with me (which they did, probably because I posed no threat and became familiar as I walked through their domain every day). In the garden with me, they behaved like any pet dog, putting a gentle paw on my leg, begging for a biscuit, or nuzzling me for affection. American Alan Beck, who pioneered research into feral dogs, believes this behavior is a "cultural camouflage." By passing themselves off as loose pets, instead of feral dogs, these canines

Plastic Bags and Potato Chips

Dogs quickly learn about plastic bags and the delicacies they contain. I once had a little black mongrel, inherited from my parents. In her former life Flossie had rarely encountered plastic garbage bags, so in the bag-lined streets of the city she walked past them, nose in the air, although they must surely have smelt tempting. It took only one walk with my friend's dog Artie, a veteran of plastic-bag opening, for Flossie to do the same—a habit she maintained until her death aged eighteen. More than this, though, a canine light bulb had gone on: Flossie loved potato chips, but had always had to have the proffered packet ripped open for her. No more! She extrapolated her wisdom of how to open the garbage bags, and now took the packets of potato chips from my hand, carefully holding them down with one paw and ripping them open with her teeth.

were more readily tolerated by the humans they encountered. However, although these two dogs clearly enjoyed my company, they quite clearly craved their freedom just as much—and why not? They were free to be dogs, to follow their own agendas, to gambol joyously with pals of their choice, to sniff messages on trees, and to wallow in muddy puddles.

Of course, most feral dogs are dependent on humans, not in the sense that we specifically cater for them, but because they need the food we supply in our garbage cans, the hiding places we create in our building works, the shelter we provide by an abandoned car (a secure place for a bitch to give birth or a comfortable back seat to relax on), and (most importantly) for us to tolerate their presence —something graphically illustrated by Alan Beck's 1970 study of the free-ranging canines of Baltimore. At their most active during the twilight hours of summer, but going about their business at all hours in cooler weather, the dogs created a flurry of activity around the neighborhood's large garbage cans. They tipped over the cans to get at the plastic and paper bags piled within, and then either dined on the spot or carried the bags back to their own secret domain where "careful rummaging" took place.

The Baltimore dogs included every variety of hound from German shepherd to tiny mongrel, who banded together in loose-knit groups, various flexible groupings, as well as tightly knit pairings, such as that of mongrel Shag and his Doberman pal, but more of them later; see pp.110–11. One consequence of this was that Beck "observed larger dogs knocking over garbage cans and making the food available for smaller dogs."

Mainstream science tries hard to discredit evidence of animals helping one another or showing compassion, but dogs, like us, are sociable creatures and, like us, need to cooperate to survive. Why should it be so surprising that they look out for one another? Dogs are loyal to their human companions, pine for them, mourn them, guard them—surely it would be extraordinary if they did not do the same for their canine friends?

Man and Beast's Best Friend

This example taken from R.H. Smythe's book *Animal Psychology*, published in 1968 and a ground-breaking book in its era, records how a lost mongrel, who had fallen into a disused mine shaft, was kept alive by her friend, a smooth-haired, fox-terrier bitch.

Dogs are loyal not only to their human keepers, but to their canine companions too. They have even been known to bring food to their friends in distress.

"The two of them had been in the habit of going off hunting together. Someone noticed that the bitch went off alone always travelling in one direction. This led us to an old mine shaft from which we could distinctly hear barking. When a rescue party descended about forty feet [about 13.5m] they found the dog on a ledge, uninjured. Also on the ledge was a fresh bone, which the owner recognized as that from a leg of mutton of the previous Sunday, together with several bread crusts. As no person visited this shaft it can only be presumed the bitch carried them to the mouth of the shaft and dropped them."

More complex emotions are revealed by the behavior of a young collie belonging to a butcher. This butcher originally had two collies, one older, one younger, who were firm friends. However, he drowned the older in the sea because the dog had become "useless through age." A few days later the drowned collie's body was washed ashore and discovered by the young dog "who was seen immediately to go to the butcher's shop and take away a piece of meat and lay it at the dead dog's mouth." (From *The Spectator Book of Dog Stories*.)

Baltimore Buddies

Back in Baltimore Beck had become particularly interested in and fond of Shag, who had a constant companion in his canine friend Dobe. Shag, having been evicted from his relatively salubrious hallway home for constant scent-marking, was now spending his nights in thick shrubbery. At 6:00AM Shag and Dobe appeared on the mean streets and made for their usual feeding alley, where they made a thorough examination of the available garbage. They lifted some choice bags from the tops of the garbage piles (even had this been garbage collection day, there was always plenty of food scattered on the ground). By 6:20AM the pair returned to a main hanging area where "as usual they found water under the air-conditioning unit." (During a particularly prolonged hot, dry period they had found a convenient, leaking fire hydrant, and also compassionate humans who had provided them with bowls of water.) The dogs then lay down for a quick nap until Dobe made off on further important dog business at 6:34AM. Five minutes later Shag woke, sniffed the air and "then immediately took off in the same direction as Dobe." At 7:10AM Shag found a garbage can on its side and devoured spaghetti, bread, and sauce, although rejected prunes, raisins, and tobacco. Clearly a dog cannot live on pasta alone and, reunited, the pair made off, stopping at another building, which they watched intently until, at 7:52AM, a woman dropped down hot dogs for Dobe and chopped meat for Shag. Replete, the dogs made for the cool of the shrubbery to sleep off breakfast. For Shag and Dobe this had been a rewarding few hours.

Beck lost sight of Shag and Dobe for six weeks and feared they had been run over or gassed. (The Society for Prevention of Cruelty to Animals performed gassing in order to keep down numbers of strays. During Beck's study (1970–1) 12,294 Baltimore dogs were taken to the gas chamber.) However, both Shag and Dobe had found homes with humans: Dobe to a desirable residence in the suburbs; while Shag remained in the city, the darling of a wealthy man, who let him out unattended in the mornings to taste his old life. He still checked out "the garbage cans along some of his old rounds," but rarely ate anything and soon returned home.

Did Shag miss Dobe? Would he have behaved differently and been tempted back to his old life had his friend still been on the streets? We will never know—but for the time being at least, it seems Shag was getting the best of both worlds and had no intention of abandoning his compassionate human.

Dogs Raising Humans

And dogs will happily extend their help to us—even if that help contains elements of self-interest. In contemporary Russia some street children have been kept alive solely through their association with dogs. In 1998 a boy, Ivan Mishukov, was forcibly separated from a group of feral dogs who had been his companions and preservers on the freezing Moscow streets for two years. Aged four, Ivan had ran away from an intolerable home and survived by begging. He had ingratiated himself with the dogs by giving them scraps of food. In return the dogs' body-heat kept him warm and the dogs themselves provided protection from malevolent humans. However, while the boy was taken to "safety," the dogs' reward was to be taken to the pound. Apparently Ivan is now "just like any other Moscow child. Yet it is said that, at night, he dreams of dogs"—the best friends he has ever known.

And this is not the only story of its kind. In a remote house in Bespalovskoya, Andrei Tolstyk, aged three months, was abandoned by his mother and soon after his father, and left to survive with only the family guard dog for care, protection, and company. The boy was discovered in August 2004 aged seven years. Other inhabitants of the village had not even known he was there. Somehow it seems that the dog had kept them both alive. Andrei is now separated from his lifelong companion, but he continues to sniff his food before eating it, is extremely reluctant to walk on two legs, and bites people. Whether he will ever totally adapt to human society remains to be seen.

Looking Out for Number One

When food is short behavior must be ruthless and the canine anti-hero of the following report displays the dog's remarkable capacity for cunning and a shrewd grip on canine psychology.

"In Regent Street [London], of all places, one bright winter morning I caught sight of a dog lying on the pavement close to the wall, hungrily gnawing a big beef bone which he had stolen or picked out of a neighbouring dust-hole. He was a miserable-looking object, a sort of lurcher of a dirty red colour, with ribs showing like the bars of a grid-iron through his mangy side ... . Presently a small red dog came trotting along the pavement from the direction of the Circus [Piccadilly Circus], and catching sight of the mangy lurcher with the bone he was instantly struck motionless, and crouching low as if to make a dash at the other, his tail stiff, his hair bristling, he continued gazing for some moments; and then, just when I thought the rush and struggle was about to take place, up jumped this little red cur and rushed back towards the Circus, uttering a succession of excited shrieky barks. The contagion was irresistible. Off went the lurcher, furiously barking too, and quickly overtaking the small dog dashed on and away to the middle of the Circus to see what all the noise was about. It was something tremendously important to dogs in general no doubt. But the little red dog, the little liar, had no sooner been overtaken and passed by the other, than back he ran, and picking up the bone, made off with it in the opposite direction. Very soon the lurcher returned and appeared astonished and puzzled at the disappearance of his bone. There I left him, still looking for it and sniffing at the open shop doors."
W.H. Hudson, *The Book of a Naturalist* (1919)

Dogs of the Laxmi Vilas Palace

In 2001 I visited Bharatpur, Rajasthan in India— a very different place culturally and physically from Baltimore, but which also teems with free-ranging canines, although all are mongrels. Death by car and wildly driven juggernaut (a large truck, the name of which derives from the Hindu god Jagannath, lord of the world) is frequent, although there are no anti-cruelty societies waiting to gas the dogs—a rather more *laissez-faire* attitude prevails in India, in neighborhoods rich and poor. Nevertheless, food is less abundant and the dogs must share it with free-ranging pigs, sacred cows, and chattering monkeys.

In Bharatpur City feral dogs are sometimes adopted by families and sit proudly outside their companion's house or open shop-front, but the majority skulk in the streets and lanes of the city, begging

Canines and Crows

Members of the crow family, like wolves and dogs, are social creatures, and as they often feast on the same prey, have developed a mutually rewarding, playful relationship. Ravens will peck the tails of wolves, who will in turn stalk the birds, who will allow the wolf oh-so close before flying off—only to repeat the fun. The dogs and crows of Bharatpur were no different, chasing one another and playing tag around their food pit.

In Rajasthan, homeless dogs feed like kings, even if they have to share supper with other beasts of the wild—such as the mischievous monkeys.

for leftovers, raiding trash cans, and drinking from dirty gutters and open sewers. Life is really hard for these dogs compared with the denizens of Baltimore (see pp.110–11), but for those who live behind the Laxmi Vilas Palace, a hotel on the fringes of town, life is considerably easier.

Eating and Drinking

As garbage collection is strictly limited in Bharatpur, the hotel burns its flammable trash, while outside its garden walls, on the edge of rough semi-cultivated farmland, a large pit takes all the considerable kitchen leftovers: free-range chicken, lamb, and goat; rice, vegetables, and naan—no junk food here, which allows the feral dogs, and their ever-present companions the house crows (see box, p.113) to feast royally.

Water is provided for the irrigation of the mustard plants by the kitchens, and if necessary the dogs can trot a few hundred yards to a small, natural stream. These hardy canines have made the food pit their headquarters and their strolls always include it. Although they are not a pack, at least in the sense of a wolf pack, these dogs maintain themselves as a fluid group, many of whom sleep together in the heat of the day. There appears to be no overall alpha dog. Instead different dogs take the lead in disparate situations and have different "jobs." For example, at the approach of strange humans, a small black dog with a curly tail immediately gets up and starts off the barking, both to keep the perceived threat at bay and to alert his group to the intruder. However, at other times this dog is subordinate to a large tan dog, who initiates food searches into the surrounding countryside.

Summer is really hot in Bharatpur, temperatures of forty degrees Celsius (approximately 105° Fahrenheit) are not uncommon, and by day the pack sleep or take a convenient snack from the food pit—all the dogs are a good weight and they have strong, white teeth and sweet breath. But regardless of the fact that there is an excess of high-quality protein in the pit, by the cool of the night ancient instincts rise and the dogs mass to hunt. Beck reports that the Baltimore dogs sometimes killed rats and ground-nesting birds. The Akita who runs with my dog Poppy often kills moles. Incredibly, he locates them as they near the surface of the earth and defeats them with one sure pounce. However, for the Akita the hunt is enough—he leaves his prey for Poppy, who gratefully gulps down his offering in one.

In Bharatpur pickings are much richer and one evening the group even dragged back a water-buffalo calf: I had heard the group hunting on the previous night, but they had moved too far too fast for me to watch their kill (if that was, in fact, what it was—but certainly, apart from the familiar house crows, and later the vultures, no other carnivores laid claim to the carcass). In 24 hours not even a sliver of bone remained—just four hooves and a scrap of hide.

Honorary Members Welcome

Honorary group members are two disabled dogs. One has bad palsy, the other a growth the size of a football attached to his leg. Although wolf experts report that pack-members displaying unusual physical problems are often killed, the palsy dog, small, black, and constantly shaking, always slept with the group and was never hassled when she ate at the pit. The dog with the tumor was an outsider, always several feet away from the group, but he also was allowed to partake freely of the bounty of the pit and the other dogs never showed him the least bit of aggression.

I, too, was permitted to wander at will through their midst, and even to examine the contents of their pit, but my affection was never solicited. Some would take a biscuit from my hand but return immediately to their canine companions. They seemed to have no desire to become more intimately entwined with humans—and why should they? They have everything they need, and live in a kind of canine Eden.

The princeliest dog at the Laxmi Vilas Palace Hotel is Gypsy, who sleeps soundly at the foot of his master's bed.

Official Dogs of the Laxmi Vilas Palace

There are also three official canine residents of the Laxmi Vilas Palace: Gypsy, Leli, and Lela. Top of the dog social tree is royal Gypsy. A handsome black Labrador, belonging to the hotel's owner Deepraj Singh, Gypsy lives in the palace, sleeps at the foot of his master's bed, and dines on roast lamb and goat. Friendly and lovable as only a labrador knows how, Gypsy is everyone's favorite. His coat gleams with health and at the least indication of malaise he is rushed to the vet. Walked several times a day by his own personal guard, Gypsy lacks for nothing except the freedom to behave like a dog—for Gypsy has failed to negotiate a diplomatic treaty with the feral dogs with whom he fights. They are many, he but one. His whole body bursts with pent-up energy and the desire to gambol and run, but Gypsy may never enjoy being free.

Leli and Lela are two mongrels who belong to the hotel-owner's father but unlike Gypsy they and the feral dogs have developed a *modus operandi* involving strict demarcation zones. If either side breaches these borders, skirmishes occur. This canine negotiation means that Leli and Lela can enjoy Laxmi Vilas' luxuriant gardens, enjoy fresh poppadoms, naan, and meat tikka from the hotel's *al fresco* tandoor oven, and wander in the mustard fields whenever they choose. They live the carefree life enjoyed by western pets only a few short decades ago, roaming free, playing, sleeping, and mating at will; while at the same time they are lavishly fed and taken to the vet if necessary. However, unlike Gypsy, who is utterly dependent upon Leli and Lela, they are aloof with people, even their caretaker, although they are pet enough to submit to being stroked if they must.

Every Dog Has Its Own Agenda

Dogs know perfectly well what they should or should not do in human terms, but naturally this does not always coincide with their own desires and agendas. Many dogs, including my own dog Poppy, only pay lip service to our rules. I can hear outraged dog-trainers everywhere chorusing: "If she had trained that dog it would do as it was told." I have to say that I do not dispute this, but I, at least, am happy for my dog to express herself.

How many humans, time after time, return to find their dog apparently snoring peacefully in her basket, her illicit relaxation on the sofa given away only by a soft curve in the cushion or a stray hair on the upholstery? Will they ever come home and actually discover their dog on the sofa? No. The dog is far too clever for that—but not clever enough to plump up the cushions.

Researchers at the Max Planck Institute in Leipzig placed tempting treats on the floor and forbade their canine charges to eat them. The dogs duly obeyed— until, that is, the

Your dog may feign innocence, but leave temptation within the reach of her paws and as soon as your back is turned ....

117

Displacement Activity in Dogs

Poppy hates my whirring, erratically moving vacuum cleaner, but knows that she should not attack it. Nevertheless she hides behind the door, and then, unable to contain herself, leaps unexpectedly on the large flat suction nozzle. Another ploy is to walk past the machine as if unconcerned and making for the sofa, and then at the last moment execute a 360-degree turn and pounce. If this fails, she again pretends to be disinterested and when she believes, correctly, that I am preoccupied with the cleaning, she walks casually past the machine again and launches an attack on the vacuum cleaner's body—an act that inevitably makes me furious. Poppy, prevented from making her attack, but simply unable to control her passionate hatred of the vacuum cleaner, then rushes into the kitchen and starts furiously eating her dinner—I always leave something in her bowl: her very own displacement activity.

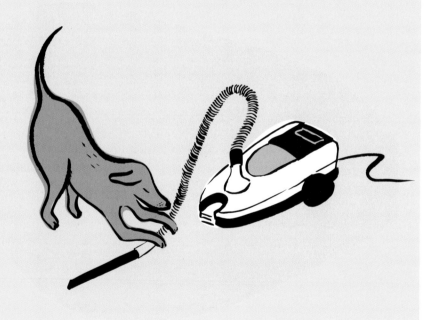

researchers left the room. Once the researchers were out of sight, the dogs scoffed the food in less than five seconds. However, if the researchers stayed in the room for a while, the dogs adopted a thieving strategy dependent on the human's behavior. "If someone was keeping an eye on the dog, then in 75 percent of cases when the food was taken, the dog would take an indirect approach—wandering around the room before gobbling it up." In other words the dog tried to fool the researcher as to their true intent. If the researcher was playing a computer game, so their attention was not directed toward the dog at all, the dog bothered with this subterfuge only 24 percent of the time.

The hyena, another member of the carnivora family and a not-so-distant relative of the dog, is a master of deception—to a point. Take, for example, the hyena in the following story: He clearly knew his group would disapprove of his actions, but the temptation was irresistible. A cow's head, thoroughly delicious should you be a hyena, lay awaiting discovery in a zoo enclosure. One male, coming across it before his compatriots, dashed away with the head into a cool pool and sat upon it without a care in the world. The other hyenas arrived and soon realized that, even if it were not there now, a new supply of food had been there very recently. The top female plunged into the pool, put her head underwater and spied the head. She surfaced, grabbed the greedy hyena by the scruff of his neck and delivered the prize feast to the rest of the group. Furthermore she punished the arch deceiver by preventing him from devouring even one morsel. Crafty, but like his canine cousins, this hyena was not quite crafty enough.

CHAPTER SEVEN:

HOW YOUR DOG HELPS AND HEALS YOU

"Dogs are our link to paradise. They don't know evil or jealousy or discontent. To sit with a dog on a hillside on a glorious afternoon is to be back in Eden, where doing nothing was not boring—it was peace."

Milan Kundera (1929–present)

Since the most ancient of times the dog and the wolf have protected and guided us both in their earthly corporeal form and as zoomorphic divinities. In this chapter we look at how the dog and its ancestors have been revered and loved throughout time; and how that human devotion has been repaid through countless selfless acts by dogs themselves. A key component in the way our dogs "talk" to us is by their actions-from offering companionship and a warm body to stroke for stress-relief, to healing the sick and rescuing those in danger.

One of the world's first-known gods is the Egyptian Wepwawet (the "Opener of the Ways"), said to guide the spirits of the dead through barren deserts to the sanctuary of the Kingdom of Osiris (in Egyptian myth Osiris was the first king on earth and, after his death, the ruler of the underworld). Wepwawet is often depicted in canine form—as a jackal, or jackal-headed man.

In Ancient Egypt jackals lived on the fringes of the deserts and their tracks between oases showed travelers a safe path through an unforgiving landscape. Wepwawet's sanctuary was at Lycopolis ("Wolf City"), a name given to the city of Syut during Hellenistic times. Wolves also inhabited Ancient Egypt and Wepwawet was often represented with a wolf-like gray or white head.

Stylized representation in Ancient Egyptian art, and confusion in nomenclature by the Egyptians themselves, and later the Greeks, has led to uncertainty over exactly which canine was representing Wepwawet. But that Wepwawet was a canid of some sort is not surprising. Some Egyptologists have noted that domestic canines were devoted to their masters, even to death, and loyally defended their property and person. It seems natural, then, that these ancients should choose a doggish creature to be their guide, and their judge, as they made their way to the realms of the spirit.

In time Wepwawet became associated with the jackal-headed god Anubis, and was often depicted leading the dead toward his Hall of Judgment. In this room Wepwawet/Anubis weighed the heart of the deceased against a feather that represented truth, justice, and goodness. The statue of Anubis discovered in the tomb of Tutenkamun, with its prominent hip bones, noticeable loins, up-stretched neck, and alert head, is claimed by their admirers to be that most venerable of breeds the Saluki (see pp.18–19), but the truth has died with the statue's sculptor.

By the Egyptian Greco-Roman period (332 BC–AD 395), Anubis had become Hermanubis, the Alexandrian dog deity, commonly known as Latrator, or "The Barker." Although he too conducted the souls of the dead through the Underworld, Hermanubis was associated with masculine sexual prowess, frequently invoked in love charms, and a powerful protector of pregnant women. At the height of his cult, Hermanubis was worshiped by thousands upon thousands at the Anoubeion of Alexandria, where his painted, dressed, and perfumed effigy was displayed in the outer courtyard. From Egypt, the cult of the dog quickly spread through Italy to Greece and became centered at Cynopolis—"Dog City"—where veneration extended to the city's entire canine population. The dogs were ritually fed with food provided by the city's humans.

These hieroglyphs reveal how Egyptian dogs were integral to hunting, religion, and the home.

Dogs as Doctors

As well as the afterlife, canines were associated with healing. Anubis was the physician to the Egyptian pantheon. In ancient Greece dogs were sacred to the sun god and healing divinity Apollo; while Apollo's son Asklepios, physician to the gods and patron of medicine, was frequently represented with dogs (and snakes). Canines symbolically represented light and thus the return of life from death—being cured.

Is there a doctor in the house? If you are a dog-owner then yes. Since ancient times dogs have been credited with the ability to detect and even cure illness.

Asklepios's divine power effected miraculous cures at his temple at Epidaurus (in the modern-day Peloponnese), where merely to dream of him was to ensure healing. One source writes that "Pamphaeos, suffering from festering abscesses in his mouth dreamed that the god held open his mouth and cleansed it; when he awoke, he was cured."

But the god also acted directly through his sacred, flesh-and-blood, temple dogs. One temple inscription reports that "A dog has cured a boy from Aigina. He had a growth on his neck. When he came to the god, one of the sacred dogs treated him while he was awake with his tongue and made him well." Another records that "Thuson of Hermione, a blind boy, had his eyes licked in the daytime by one of the dogs about the temple and departed cured."

Dogs That Heal

The ancient Greeks were not the only people to credit dog saliva with healing properties. The Bible recounts how Lazarus's sores were healed after having been licked by a dog. In addition a letter to *The Lancet* in the mid-1900's reports that Fijian fishermen heal their lacerations by encouraging their pet dogs to lick them. Doctor Rover, a canine belonging to Reverend Egerton R. Young, a Missionary in Canada at the turn of the century, healed his canine companion's galls, wounds, and frozen feet by spontaneously licking them. Those the dog was unable to reach failed to improve. Referring to Rover in his article "Medical discoveries by the Non-medical," George M. Gould MD comments that this shows that "in a state of good health and with pure food the dog's saliva has a perfect bactericidal and healing power. Perhaps it would make a good antiseptic. No bacteriologist has caught the hint."

Almost a hundred years later the medical world is beginning, finally, to catch on. In 1990 Hart and Powell working in the US discovered that canine saliva was bactericidal against E. Coli, a pathogen found in feces and responsible for food poisoning in humans, and enteritis in newly born puppies—both of which can be fatal. It also acted against *Streptococcus canis*, which together with E. coli causes septicemia in pups. So when the pups' mother licks her nipples, and undertakes genital grooming on herself and her pups, she is keeping them all free from disease. Both these pathogens are also commonly present in wounds—so clearly it makes sense to lick them too.

Dr. Nigel Benjamin, a pharmacologist at St. Bartholomew's Hospital in London and at the London School of Medicine and Dentistry, has more recently discovered that the components of both dog and human saliva oxidize on contact with flesh, producing nitric oxide—an extremely powerful antimicrobial substance. Benjamin is now working on treating infectious skin diseases using the same compound.

The Dog as Diagnostician

Dogs may also be diagnosticians. Writing in *The Lancet* in 2001, Church and Williams, physicians at the Queens Medical Centre, Nottingham (UK), describe the case of a 66-year-old man who developed a patch of eczema on his thigh, which over the course of 18 years grew to be a little less than one inch (about 2cm) in diameter. In 1994 the man purchased Parker, a labrador. In 1999 Parker began to "persistently push his nose against his owner's trouser leg, sniffing the lesion beneath it." On his labrador's advice the man went to his doctor and the lesion, which turned out to be

A Cure for Psoriasis?

In 2004 a man who had had psoriasis on more than fifty percent of his body for many years and had tried virtually every available treatment wrote "I also have a silly habit of letting my dog lick my feet. My feet had two small patches of psoriasis a few weeks back, the dog licked them, I find it to be quite a lazy way of scratching my sores. But, to my amazement, the psoriasis patches on my feet all cleared up. I proceeded to let the dog lick a spot on my elbow and it's clearing up, too. 'Doggy! Come lick my back!' My friends are pondering if the enzymes in my dog's saliva aren't the cure."

Fijian fishermen healed their lacerations (an unfortunate occupational hazard) by allowing their dogs to lick the wounds.

cancerous, was duly cut out. Parker no longer sniffs the area.

Since the first early reports of the dog's ability to sense illness, clinics have begun to train dogs specifically to detect a number of different cancers. One such canine is Shing Ling-hua, a beautiful and intelligent, pure-bred, apricot-colored standard poodle whose Chinese name romantically means "essence of apricot flower": She is named after Apricot Grove in China, where more than two thousand years ago a benevolent herbalist refused to accept money from his patients and asked only that they plant apricot trees in his mountain meadow.

In 2001 researchers at the Pine Street Chinese Benevolent Association's medical clinic in Northern California, where Shing Ling-hua works, formed a partnership with Dr. James Walker, director of the Sensory Research Institute at Florida State University. Walker is researching the early detection of cancer by identifying chemical markers of the disease in exhaled breath. The saliva, urine, and breath of individuals suffering from the very first, otherwise undetectable, signs of diseases such as lung cancer, breast cancer, liver cancer, melanoma, and heart disease, all contain odorous chemicals such as n-pentane, aldehydes, alkanes, and formaldehyde. These are the result of free-radical activity and lipid peroxidation that degrade polyunsaturated fatty acids in the body's cell membranes. As these chemicals pass through the lung's alveolar capillaries during normal circulation they are volatilized into the breath. Called volatile organic chemicals (VOCs), they can be detected by scent.

Dubbed a "natural pet scan," Shing Ling-hua has been trained to recognize these VOCs and so detect cancers long before they show up on an X-ray. Her wonderful abilities also are also helping Dr. Walker to develop an "electronic nose," which, one day, may be as accurate as Shing Ling-hua herself.

Dogs as Confidants and Companions

Wonderful as the canine's medical abilities are they are nothing compared with its ability to alleviate human loneliness, depression, bereavement, and physical pain. In cancer wards throughout the world, there are thousands of children undergoing long and painful treatment. One study of children who were having drugs put directly into their veins through implanted ports, found that the experience was much less physically painful and emotionally stressful for them if a real live dog were there with them.

Whereas people may judge others, or simply be reluctant to take on another's problems, dogs are willing, discreet, and nonjudgmental confidants. Because of these attributes, and their warm, tactile presence, dogs are able to break even the most terrible cycles of human helplessness and social isolation. Central London has its fair share of the homeless, the addicted, and the mentally ill walking its streets. Often, these people, who a moment before might have been shouting to no one, waving their arms around, or weaving down the street, stop when they see my dog Poppy. They ask if they can stroke her and, as they do so, they become quite gentle, different people. Their eyes light up and for a brief moment they perhaps feel part of the wider world (see pp.73–4). After all, they have not only touched a living creature, but spoken to another human being because of her.

Therapists are now beginning to realize how useful this "icebreaking" ability is. They are increasingly using pets when dealing with abnormally withdrawn or antisocial patients—a trend started by Sigmund Freud, but perhaps more for his benefit than that of his patients. Suffering terribly from cancer, analysis became

In Praise of the Newfoundland

As Emily Dickinson learned no breed could be a more devoted companion than the heroic and august Newfoundland. His character is illustrated perfectly in this charming nineteenth-century children's song:

I am the noble Newfoundland
My voice is deep and loud
I keep watch all through the night
While other people sleep

(From *The Mythology of Dogs: canine legend and lore through the ages*, G. Houseman and L. Houseman, St. Martins Press, New York, 1997.)

somewhat tiresome for Freud so he employed Jofi, his devoted chow, to be a second pair of ears for his patients—but nevertheless one with an eye on the clock. Jofi signaled the end of every session with copious yawning and stretching, never allowing Freud to exceed the statutory hour by even one minute. The chow also comforted Freud through the excruciating operations in his mouth, "I wish you could have seen with me what sympathy Jofi shows me during these hellish days, as if she understood everything," wrote Freud gratefully in 1936 to his friend Marie Bonaparte.

Without her Newfoundland Carlo, who helped her transform mental turmoil into exceptional writing, Emily Dickinson might never have become one of America's most distinguished poets. A highly-strung, anxious woman, Dickinson found even day-to-day social commerce excruciating. So much so that by her thirties she rarely went out and she received no one. Dickinson relied on bearlike Carlo to soothe her disquiet, make her feel safe, and act as a go-between. When suffering from heartache, yet unable to express her passion directly, Dickinson wrote to the object of her affection: "I tell you Mr. Bowles, it is a Suffering, to have a sea—no care how Blue—between your Soul and you—and the puzzled look deepens in Carlo's forehead as the Days go by and you never Come?" In another letter, to the editor of the *Amherst College Paper*, she describes the dog's protective qualities thus: "Don't be afraid of [a metaphor], sir, it won't bite. If it was my Carlo now! The Dog is the noblest work of Art Sir — his mistress's rights he doth defend—although it bring him to his end."

Carlo gave Dickinson the unconditional love and protection she desperately needed. In her poetry we learn that Dickinson considered Carlo and the natural world to be "Better than Being—Because they know—but do not tell", while people "talk of Hallowed things aloud—and embarrass my dog." That Carlo must have been invaluable to Dickinson is shown by her genuine and unselfish love for him. In 1863, suffering from severe eye problems and unable to read or write, she was forced to leave home to undergo treatment in Boston. Instead of thinking of herself and demanding that Carlo come with her, she insisted that her true and faithful friend stay at home "because that he would die, in Jail."

Dogs as Our Saviors

The Newfoundland is the strongest of the water dogs and possesses webbed paws and a water-resistant double coat. As a result she has been helping and saving humans for centuries. Often employed at sea, she worked with sailors by retrieving cargo or valuables that fell overboard, and by swimming to land with a line in stormy weather. Sadly these brave dogs all-too-often lost their lives in the line of duty—although Rigel, hero of the *Titanic*, did not.

Rigel, who belonged to the first officer of the *Titanic*, stayed on board until the ship sank. He then plunged into the icy waters to seek his master. Meanwhile the *SS Carpathia* was speeding toward the *Titanic*, but in the dark its crew did not see that their vessel was bearing down on a lifeboat full of survivors too exhausted to attract their attention. Intelligent Rigel swam between the lifeboat and the *SS Carpathia* barking loudly. (Newfoundlands have an extremely deep and loud bark.) The captain of the SS *Carpathia* heard Rigel's barking and switched off his engines. Rigel then guided the lifeboat to safety, and was taken on board, apparently in fine form.

Newfoundlands can also be trained to rescue swimmers in difficulty, and they even now patrol beaches in some parts of the world. If the person is conscious, the Newfoundland will swim out beyond him or her, then turn and swim back alongside them, facing in the direction of land. This way the person is able to grab the Newfoundland and allow the dog to tow them in. If unconscious, a Newfoundland will grasp the swimmer's upper arm in his mouth, causing the person to roll onto his back so that his head is above the water, and thus bring him back to shore to safety.

A Newfoundland is said to have saved some of the survivors of the Titanic by attracting the attention of a rescue boat.

But sometimes Newfoundlands can be overzealous in carrying out their duties, as shown in this piece taken from the UK's *The Times* dated September 14, 1839.

"While a gentleman was bathing yesterday morning in the Serpentine river, in Hyde Park [London], he nearly met with his death under the following singular circumstances. It appears that Mr Ashton, tailor of No. 17 Pall Mall, is in possession of a very large and sagacious Newfoundland dog, and the gentleman, who is a friend of Mr Ashton's took the dog with him on going to bathe ... . The animal, seeing the gentleman swimming about in the water, supposed he was drowning, swam directly to the spot, seized the hair of his head, and, elevating his head considerably above the water, proceeded to drag him towards the shore ... . The gentleman resisted and this strange contest continued for some minutes in the water until the gentleman was quite exhausted. An alarm was raised and the men belonging to the Humane Society ... arrived just in time to save him ... he was conveyed to his residence in a coach, accompanied by his over-zealous canine companion."

And Finally...

Dogs occupy a unique niche on the border between human cultural construct and wild nature. This enables them to act as ambassadors for the animal kingdom, re-introducing us to the natural world of which we are a part—not apart. Carlo gave Dickinson (see p.128) the freedom to commune with nature as she wondered alone, except for "Hills—Sir and the sundown and a dog—large as myself," and research constantly shows that children who have good relationships with pets develop an overall sense of humanity and a true love of all nature.

Dogs also help in the practical fight to conserve what is left of our ever-dwindling wildlife. In 2001 a rescue dog—a sassy mongrel called Charlie—and a svelte, blond, family labrador, named Blair were trained by the British army, not to sniff out explosives or cocaine, but ivory. They are now in Kenya where, accompanied by two handlers and a team of Masai warrior game rangers, they are sniffing out contraband ivory in airplanes and baggage at Nairobi airport, and discovering caches of ivory buried deep in the bush. To get them used to the wildlife of Africa, the dogs were introduced to cows. However, nothing could prepare them for their first walk through a herd of giraffes when, according to Lt. Corporal Duke, "their eyes nearly popped out of their heads."

Humankind has many personal and environmental difficulties at this time and the reason for so many of them are "his inability to come to terms with his inner self and to harmonize his culture with his membership in the world of nature." (Levinson, *Pets and Human Nature*). Perhaps, then, it is not too farfetched to think that if we open our hearts and listen to what our dog is saying, the canine ambassador could indeed be our savior.

Man Saves Dog

Cyril LaBreque was on his schooner with his 80-pound (36-kg) labrador, Happer, when the boat began to sink. Happer and his master made it to the lifeboat while the two unfortunate crew could only cling to the gunwales, and eventually drowned.

LaBreque was charged with manslaughter for refusing to throw Happer overboard to make room for the men. He countered that Happer was too heavy for him to lift and that, anyway, the boat would have capsized had he been able to throw him into the sea. In May 1974 a New Jersey jury found LaBreque ... NOT GUILTY!

GLOSSARY: The Top 50 Dog Breeds

Labrador:
The most popular breed in the United States, the Labrador was bred originally as a retriever but has the perfect temperament for a family pet.

Golden Retriever:
A top obedience competition winner, it is also used as a guide for the blind, a therapy dog, and service dog for the disabled as well as a family pet.

Beagle:
A hardy, short-coated hound, the Beagle is a fine companion with a gentle, happy disposition, despite being originally bred in packs.

German Shepherd Dog:
Handsome and strong, this breed is also known as the Alsatian. A favorite working dog, it is intelligent and loyal.

Dachshund:
Standing on short legs with an elongated body, all sizes of this ancient German breed of hound are affectionate and curious.

Yorkshire Terrier:
The country's favorite miniature breed stands only 6 inches (12cm) tall. It has a long and silky coat and a courage above its stature.

Boxer:
Compact and strong, the boxer has a short, shiny, brown and white coat. Although very energetic, it forms deep bonds with families, especially children.

Poodle:
Whether Toy, Miniature, or Standard, this French breed has a thick, curly coat and a bouncy step. Companionable and good-natured, they are especially good with children.

Shih Tzu:
Originally bred in the Forbidden City in Beijing, this small Tibetan breed is covered in a soft double coat of long hair.

Chihuahua:
This tiny dog from Mexico is the oldest breed in the Americas and the smallest in the world. It is famous for its large ears.

Miniature Schnauzer:
A German terrier named after the word for "muzzle," it is square-bodied and bushy-haired with a long snout.

Pug:
This small Asian breed is nearly 2,500 years old. Square and compact, moles on the face are considered to be beauty spots.

Pomeranian:

Tiny and fluffy with sharp, upright ears, it is intelligent and friendly, has a loud bark, and will, stand up to much larger dogs.

Cocker Spaniel:

With long ears and a soft, silky coat, this compact gundog is also an inseparable companion.

Rottweiler:

This natural guard dog has a massive, powerful body and is both calm and courageous, despite its somewhat fearsome reputation.

Bulldog:

Small and compact with a massive head and drooping cheeks, this British mastiff can be gentle despite its breeding.

Shetland Sheepdog:

This long-haired collie is strong and lightly built. It is loyal and gentle, while also eminently trainable.

Boston Terrier:

Originally a fighting dog, this short-haired, large-eared terrier has been bred into a gentle, well-mannered dog.

Miniature Pinscher:

This sleek, black-and-tan terrier, which is unrelated to the Doberman, can be willful and high spirited.

Maltese:

Known to the ancient Greeks, this toy dog is famous for its luxurious silky white coat.

German Shorthaired Pointer:

Energetic, cheerful, and famed for its hunting skills, this breed needs a lot of space to exercise.

Doberman Pinscher:

Powerful though elegant, this black-and-tan breed has a fearsome reputation as a guard dog.

Siberian Husky:

The ideal working dog for the frozen North, this thick-coated Husky is most famous for pulling sleds.

Pembroke Welsh Corgi:

Originating in the Welsh region of Pembrokeshire, the breed is closely associated with its most famous owner and breeder, the British Queen Elizabeth II.

Basset Hound:

Long-bodied with a large head, the Basset can be stubborn but will always remain friendly.

Bichon Frise:

This friendly ball of white hair is a relative of the poodle, though is not known as a barker.

Great Dane:

A giant up to three feet (1m-) high, with short, close-fitting hair, it was originally bred to overcome bears.

English Springer Spaniel:

A compact and gentle sporting dog that is an ideal family pet, even though it is highly energetic.

Weimaraner:

A beautiful and sleek German hunting dog, the Weimaraner has a smooth, short gray or brown coat and lives happily among the family.

Brittany:

In looks, similar to, though a little heavier than, the Springer, the Brittany is intelligent and easy to handle.

West Highland White Terrier:

A hardy and compact dog with bright, dark eyes and a thick, white coat which was bred from the Cairn Terrier.

Collie:

Made famous by Lassie, this long-coated Scottish sheepdog has a justified reputation for intelligence.

Mastiff:

One of the heaviest breeds at up to 200lbs (91kg) this English breed of fierce guard dog was known to the Romans.

Australian Shepherd:

An American herding dog, despite its name, that is affectionate and loyal, though perhaps too energetic to be an ideal pet.

Cavalier King Charles Spaniel:

A small and affectionate, large-eyed spaniel that was developed to match dogs seen in portraits of the 17th-century English king.

Papillon:

A tiny toy spaniel with a curled, plumed tail, the Papillon is one of the oldest breeds, widespread in Italy during the Renaissance.

Pekingese:

Venerated in China as demi-Gods, these toy dogs have long, silky, flowing coats and small, wrinkled muzzles.

Lhasa Apso:

From the Himalayan kingdom of Tibet, this small watchdog has a luxuriant, heavy coat and a friendly, devoted manner.

Saint Bernard:

Famed as a mountain rescue dog, this large, strong dog was first bred in Switzerland to work in the Alpine passes.

Shar-Pei:

Originally from China, the Shar-Pei has a heavily wrinkled face surrounding a wide muzzle. They can be stubborn and require firm handling.

Chesapeake Bay Retriever:

Originally a Newfoundland-retriever cross, this powerful, muscular dog has a tight, wavy coat, and is willing though sometimes slow to learn.

Cairn Terrier:

This breed of hardy Scottish terriers with a dark shaggy coat was made famous by Toto in *The Wizard of Oz*.

Scottish Terrier:

The Scottie is a sturdy, short-legged terrier that is surprisingly agile. Playful and lovable, it can dominate a household.

Akita:

The national dog of Japan, this large hunting dog resembles the husky in both looks and uses.

Vizsla:

With beautiful, short red hair, the Vizsla is a Hungarian pointer that is also a fine retriever.

Newfoundland:

A very tall and massive, though agile, dog, the Newfoundland has a thick waterproof coat that needs daily brushing.

Bernese Mountain Dog:

A sturdy, Swiss dog with a thick, waterproof black, tan, and white coat, these dogs love children, so make ideal pets.

Bull mastiff:

An English 20th-century crossbreed, this is a tall and powerful dog with a broad, wrinkled face and a large, black nose.

Bloodhound:

Famed as a tracker, this huge but mild-mannered breed has drooping ears and wrinkled skin, giving it a somewhat mournful look.

Airedale Terrier:

One of the larger terriers, this hardy breed has a short, bristly double coat of black and tan.

BIBLIOGRAPHICAL REFERENCE

The following books, articles, and journals provided invaluable reference for the writing of this book. I am greatly indebted to their authors and I hope that you might, in turn, look up their work. (Each chapter is given its own complete listings and therefore reference duplication between chapters is intentional.)

CHAPTER ONE

Ash, E.C. *Dogs: Their History and Development (2 Volumes)*, Ayer Co Publishers (1959)

Caius, Dr. John *A Treatise on Englishe Dogges* (1576)

Catlin, George *North American Indians (Volumes I and II)*, Digital Scanning Inc. (2000)

Dale-Green, Patricia *The Lore of the Dog* (1966)

Gesner, Konrad *Natural History* (1551)

Janssen, Rosalind and Jack *Egyptian Household Animals*, Shire Publications (1989)

Leonard J., Wayne R., Wheeler, J., Valadez R., Guillen, S., Vila C. "Ancient DNA Evidence for Old World Origin of New World Dogs" *Science* (Volume 298, November 2002)

Lopez, Barry *Of Wolves and Men*, Simon and Schuster (1982)

Moffet, Cleaveland "Wild Beasts and their Keepers: How The Animals in a Menagerie are Tamed Trained and Cared for" *McClures Magazine* (May 1984)

Osborn, D.J. with Osbornova, Jana *Mammals of Ancient Egypt*, Aris and Phillips (1998)

Topsell, E. *Elizabethan Zoo*, Frederick Etchells and Hugh MacDonald (1926)

Trut, Lyudmila "Early Canid Domestication: The Farm-Fox Experiment" *American Scientist* (Volume 87, March–April 1999)

Waters, David *The Saluki in History, Art and Sport*, Atlantic Books (1995)

Wayne, Robert K. "Molecular evolution of the dog family" *Trends in Genetics* (Vol. 9, June 1993)

Wayne, Robert K. and Ostrander, Elaine "Origin, Genetic Diversity, and Genome Structure of the Domestic Dog" *Bio Essays 21* (pp.247–257)

CHAPTER TWO

Black, H. and Green, J.S. "Navajo use of Mixed-breed Dogs for Management of predators" *Journal of Range Management* (Volume 38, January 1985)

Coppinger, L. and Coppinger, R. "Differences in the Behavior of Dog Breeds" in *Genetics and the Behavior of Domestic Animals* edited by Temple Grandin, San Diego (1998)

Coppinger, L. and Coppinger, R. *Dogs for Herding and Guarding*

Grandin, T. (ed.) *Livestock Handling and Transport*, CAB International (2000)

Serpell, James (ed.) *The Domestic Dog: its Evolution, Behaviour and Interactions with People*, Cambridge University Press (1995)

CHAPTER THREE

Bekoff, Marc *Minding Animals*, Oxford University Press (2002)

Budiansky, Stephen *The Truth About Dogs*, Viking (2000)

Coren, Stanley *How to Speak Dog*, Free Press (2000)

Fogle, Bruce *The Secret Life of Dog Owners*, Penguin (1998)

Fudge, Erika *Animal*, Reaktion (2002)

Hall, R. *Animals are Equal*, Wildwood House (1981)

Hare, B., Brown M., Williamson, C., and Tomasello M. "The Domestication of Social Cognition in Dogs," *Science* (Volume 298, November 2002)

Kaminski, J., Call J., and Fischer, J. "Word Learning in a Domestic Dog: Evidence for 'Fast Mapping'," *Science* (Volume 304, June 2004)

Masson, Jeffrey *Dogs Never Lie About Love*, Three Rivers Press (1998)

Mech, L. David and Boitani, Luigi (eds.) *Wolves: Behavior, Ecology, and Conservation*, University of Chicago Press (2003)

Proceedings of The International Aviculturists Society, Jan. 11–15, 1995

Sanders, Clinton R. "The Impact of Guide Dogs on the Identity of People with Visual Impairments" *Anthrozoös* (Volume 13 [2], 2000)

Spectator, The *The Spectator Book of Dog Stories* (1894)

Zimen, Erik *The Wolf, a Species in Danger*, Delacorte Press (1981)

CHAPTER FOUR

Hourdebaigt, Jean-Pierre *Canine Massage, A Complete Reference Manual*, 2nd edition, Dogwise Publishing (2004)

Jorgenson, J. "Therapeutic Use of Companion Animals in Health Care" *Image—The Journal of Nursing Scholarship* (Volume 29 [3], pp.249–254, 1997)

Lamm Esordi, Renee *You Have a Visitor*, Blue Lamm Publishing (2000)

Lynch, James J. "Developing a Physiology of Inclusion: Recognising the Health Benefits of Animal Companions" published at http://www.deltasociety.org/dsx109.htm

Lynch, James J. *The Language of the Heart*, Basic Books (1986)

Tellington-Jones, Linda and Taylor, Sybil *The Tellington Touch: Holistic Approach to Training, Healing, and Communicating with Animals*, Cloudcraft Books (1994)

Wansborough, Robert K. "The Cosmetic Docking of Dog Tails" *Australian Veterinary Journal* (Volume 74, No. 1, July 1996)

Wells, D.L. and Hepper, P.G. "The Discrimination of Dog Odours by Humans" *Perception* (Volume 29, pp.111–115, 2000)

Worwood, Valerie Ann *The Fragrant Pharmacy*, Macmillan (1990)

CHAPTER FIVE

Bechterev, W. "The Direct Influence of a Person Upon the Behaviour of Animals" *Journal of Parapsychology* (Volume 13, 1949)

Bekoff, Marc *Minding Animals*, Oxford University Press (2002)

Cain, A.O. "A Study of Pets in the Family System," *New Perspectives on Our Lives with Companion Animals* edited by A.H. Katcher and A.M. Beck, University of Pennsylvania Press (1983)

Cattell, R.B., Eber, H.W., and Tatsuoka, M.M. *Sixteen Personality Factor Questionnaire* (1970)

Country Life Magazine (5 November, 1999)

Eason, Cassandra *The Psychic Power of Animals*, Cygnus Books (2003)

Fitzpatrick, Sonya *What the Animals Tell Me*, Berkley Publishing Group (2003)

Huron, David "Is Music an Evolutionary Adaptation?" in *The Cognitive Neuroscience of Music* edited by Isabelle Peretz and Robert Zatorre, Oxford University Press (2004)

O'Donnell, Elliot *Animal Ghosts or Animal Hauntings and the Hereafter (1913)*, R.A. Kessinger Publishing (2003)

O'Farrell, Valerie "Effects of Owner Personality and Attitudes on Dog Behaviour" in *The Domestic Dog* edited by James Serpell, Cambridge University Press (1995)

Podberscek, E.S. and Gosling, S.D. "Personality Research on Pets and Their Owners" in *Companion Animals and Us* edited by A.L. Podberscek, E.S. Paul, and J.A. Serpell, Cambridge University Press (2000)

Serpell, James "Creatures of the Unconscious" in *Companion Animals and Us* edited by A.L. Podberscek, E.S. Paul, and J.A. Serpell, Cambridge University Press (2000)

Sheldrake, Rupert *The Sense of Being Stared At*, Crown (2003)

Sherwood, S.J. "Black Dog Apparitions" *Journal of the American Society for Psychical Research* (Volume 94 [3–4], pp.151–164, July–October 2000)

Trainor, L.J. and Schmidt, L.A. "Processing Emotions Induced by Music," in *The Cognitive Neuroscience of Music* edited by Isabelle Peretz and Robert Zatorre, Oxford University Press (2004)

Wells, D.L., Graham, L., and Pepper, P.G. "The Influence of Auditory Stimulation on the Behaviour of Dogs Housed in a Rescue Shelter" *Animal Welfare* (Volume 11, pp.385–393, 2002)

Williams, J.H. *Bandoola*, Doubleday (1954)

Winer, Gerald A. and Cottrell, Jane E. "Does Anything Leave the Eye When We See? Extramission Beliefs of Children and Adults" *Current Directions in Psychological Science* (Volume 5, pp.137–42, 1996)

Winer, Gerald A. et al "Fundamentally Misunderstanding Visual Perception" *American Psychologist* (Volume 57, pp.417–24, 2002)

Woodhouse, B. *How Your Dog Thinks*, Ringpress Books (1994)

Wylder, J.E. *Psychic Pets: the Secret World of Animals*, Stonehill (1978)

CHAPTER SIX

Ash, E.C. Dogs: *Their History and Development (2 Volumes)*, Ayer Co Publishers (1959)

Bekoff, Marc *Minding Animals*, Oxford University Press (2002)

Bradshaw, J.W.S and Nott, H.M.R. "Social and Communication Behaviour of Companion Dogs" in *The Domestic Dog* edited by James Serpell, Cambridge University Press (1995)

Dresser, N. "The Horse Barmitzvah: A Celebratory Exploration of the Human–Animal bond" in *Companion Animals and Us* edited by A.L. Podberscek, E.S. Paul, and J.A. Serpell, Cambridge University Press (2000)

The Independent (UK newspaper; 4 August 2004)

Kuczaj, S. *Animal Welfare Magazine* (issue 10 supplement, s161–s173, 2001)

Lopez, Barry Holstun *Of Wolves and Men*, Touchstone (1995)

Newton, Michael *Savage Girls and Wild Boys: A History of Feral Children*, Faber and Faber (2003)

Seligman, Martin E.P. "Fall into Helplessness" *Psychology Today* (Volume 7, 1973)

Smyth, R.H. *Animal Psychology*, Charles C. Thomas, Springfield, Illinois (1961)

The Sunday Telegraph (UK newspaper; June 3 2001)

CHAPTER SEVEN

Adams, Maureen "Emily Dickinson Had a Dog: An Interpretation of the Human–Dog Bond" *Anthrozoös* (Volume 12.3, pp.132–141, 1999)

Ash, E.C. *Dogs: Their History and Development (2 Volumes)*, Ayer Co Publishers (1959)

Chernak McElroy, Susan *Animals as Teachers and Healers*, Ballatine (1998)

Church, J. and Williams, H. "Another Sniffer Dog for the Clinic?" *The Lancet* (358 (9285): 930; September 15, 2001)

Corson, S.A. and Corson, E.O. (eds.) *Ethology and Nonverbal Communication in Mental Health,* Pergamon Press (1980)

Dale-Green, Patricia *The Lore of the Dog* (1966)

Dresser, N. "The Horse Barmitzvah: A Celebratory Exploration of the Human—Animal Bond" in *Companion Animals and Us* edited by A.L. Podberscek, E.S. Paul, and J.A. Serpell, Cambridge University Press (Cambridge, 2000)

Friedmann, E., Thomas, S.A., and Eddy, T.J. "Companion Animals and Human Health" *Companion Animals and Us* edited by A.L. Podberscek, E.S. Paul, and J.A. Serpell, Cambridge University Press (Cambridge, 2000)

Hart, B.L. and Powell, K.L. "Antibacterial Properties of Saliva" *Physiology and Behaviour* (Volume 48 [3], pp.383–386, 1990)

Health and Wellness Magazine (December 2002)

Jeffreys, D. "Amazing Dog that Sniffs Out Cancer," *Daily Mail* (UK newspaper, April 22, 1997)

Johnson, T. (ed.) *Poems of Emily Dickinson*, Harvard University Press (1995)

Johnson, T. and Ward, T. (eds.) *Letters of Emily Dickinson*, Harvard University Press (1958)

Kerényi, C. *Asklepios: Archetypal Image of the Physician's Existence*, Princeton University Press (1997)

Lamm Esordi, Renee *You Have a Visitor*, Blue Lamm Publishing (2000)

Osborn, D.J. *Mammals of Ancient Egypt*, Warminster (1998)

Serpell, J.A. "Creatures of the Unconscious" in *Companion Animals and Us* edited by A.L. Podberscek, E.S. Paul, and J.A. Serpell, Cambridge University Press (2000)

Waters, David *The Saluki in History, Art and Sport*, Atlantic Books (1995)

Wells, Marjorie Joan "The Effect of Pets on Children's Stress Response During Medical Procedures" *Abstracts International Section B, Science and Engineering* (Volume 59[6-b] 2689, December 1998)

Williams, H. and Pembroke, A. "Sniffer dogs in the melanoma clinic?" *The Lancet* (1 (8604): 734; 1989)

Every effort has been made to list accurate data for the entries in this reference. The Publishers and the Author apologise for any inaccuracies or omissions, all of which are unintentional. We shall, if informed, correct future editions of this bibliography.

ACKNOWLEDGMENTS

The author would like to thank: all the staff of the British Library, and particularly those patient denizens of Science Two, South, without whom this book simply would not have happened; Cindy Richards, my perspicacious publisher; and Margaret Wray, who tends faithfully to Poppy.

The author also gives thanks to A.L.J. Taylor, Head Behaviorist of Battersea Dog's Home; Breed Co-ordinator Nicola; Sealy Breame at Malamute Rescue, Mrs Taylor Smith and Penny Evans of Husky Rescue; Mrs Brazers and Mrs Walker of Samoyed Rescue; Andrew Holland at PetSounds; The Kennel Club; The American Kennel Club; and every one of my friends who talked about their dogs and kindly listened to me talk about my book.

Information on massage taken from *Canine Massage, A Complete Reference Manual*, 2nd edition by Jean Pierre Hourdebaigt (Dogwise Publishing, 2004) used with permission. Available from www.dogwise.com.

Photographs reproduced by kind permission of the author, p.15;
Creative Image Library, pp.17, 22, 70, 102, 120;
Thompson Animal Photography, pp. 6, 38, 86.
Cover photographs © Creative Image Library

INDEX